D0276822

The Little Book
of
EPITAPHS

The Little Book
of
EPITAPHS

Edited by

ESME HAWES

SIENA

This edition published and distributed by Siena, 1999

Siena is an imprint of Parragon

Parragon
Queen Street House
4 Queen Street
Bath BA1 1HE

Produced by Magpie Books, an imprint of
Robinson Publishing Ltd, London

ISBN 0 75252 858 0

A copy of the British Library Cataloguing-in-Publication Data
is available from the British Library
Printed in China

Contents

Introduction

The enduring fascination with epitaphs lies in the momentary glimpse they offer into another person's life. Generally, they are composed by ordinary people about ordinary people but with the very particular caveat that these "ordinary" folk were beloved. There is a second kind of epitaph – written not so much as a memento to the deceased but as a tribute to its author. While neither type can be treasured for its reliability, all epitaphs can be appreciated for their sincerity and they are all, in their own way, equally revelatory about the values and belief systems that they encapsulate.

The earliest epitaphs in English date from the Reformation. Instead of the formula "Pray for the soul of" which had been used up to that time, it soon became standard practice to say something about the deceased and to extol his or her virtues. Epitaphs moved with the times and, while the 16th and 17th centuries brought florid and over-effusive praise, the 18th century brought wit and Enlightenment. The 19th saw an increase in inhibition and pomposity and the 20th has embraced cremation. Brevity has, therefore, become the key.

Some were written cynically; most turned a blind eye to their subject's flaws, and yet, throughout the centuries, we can enjoy epitaphs both for the people they commemorate and for the way in which they are commemorated.

Chapter 1

DEARLY BELOVED

The vast majority of epitaphs simply express the grief and loss that humans feel when someone close to them dies. Sincere and generally uncomplicated, these are testaments to private sorrow. Most remember close family members, but there are also best friends in this section and loyal servants and even household pets — anyone, in fact, who was once, and still is, loved.

Flight Lieutenant R.V. How
(1914–44)

~

To know him was to love him.
Always in our thoughts.
Olive and David.

Elizabeth Quinton
(1762–1801)
St George, Hatley St George

~

Her most afflicted Husband John W Quinton
Whom she rendered during 23 years
the happiest of mankind,
Has placed this inscription to bear testimony
of his Gratitude to her
and his admiration
for her innumerable
Virtues,
and of his most tender and affectionate love
For her

(Intending when it shall please God to release
Him from his misery and call him from the World)
To be deposited with her in the same tomb;
And hoping that his merciful God will consider
The severe blow which it hath pleased
his Divine Will to inflict upon him
in taking from him
The dearest, the most beloved
and the most faithful
And affectionate Companion that ever blessed Man,
Together with the weight of his succeeding sorrows
As an expiation of his past offences,
And that he will grant him his grace so to live
As that he may,
through his Divine Mercy
And through the precious intercession
Of our blessed Lord and Saviour Jesus Christ
Hope for the blessing of being soon united
With her in eternal happiness.

Thomas Tipper
(1731-85)
George IV's brewer

~

To the memory of
Thomas Tipper, who
departed this life May the 14,
1785, Aged 54 years.

READER, with kind regard this grave survey,
Nor heedless pass where TIPPER'S ashes lay.
Honest he was, ingenuous, blunt, and kind;
And dared do, what few dare do, speak his mind.
PHILOSOPHY and HISTORY well he knew,
Was versed in PHYSIC and in SURGERY too.

The best old STINGO he both brewed and sold
Nor did one knavish act to get his Gold.
He played through Life a varied comic part
And knew immortal HUDIBRAS by heart.
READER, in real truth, such was the Man:
Be better, wiser, laugh more if you can.

Elizabeth Noke
(died 1658)

~

Duty while a child, love and care when a wife;
Courtesy and charity and a harmless life,
True piety to God: this shining seaven
Thro Jesus merits took her soul to heaven.

Erland d'Abo
(1911–76)
St Andrew, West Wratting

~

A romantic at heart to whom home at West Wratting
was all.
God bless him.

Wife of Sir Albert Morton
(16th century)

~

He first deceased; she for a little tried
To live without him, liked it not, and died.

Tom Richardson
(died 1912)
Surrey and England cricketer

~

He bowled his best but was himself bowled by the
best on July 2nd 1912.

Mary Sharpe
(1771–1809)
St Mary, Burwell

~

Come all my Friends you see me die for I am broken-
    hearted
Not a wish had I to live since from my loved one
    parted
When I am laid in my cold grave and should it be
    tomorrow
Write on my stone here lies a wife that drained a cup
    of sorrow.

Harriet Stuart Mill
(died 1858)
Wife of John Stuart Mill

~

Were there but a few hearts and intellects like hers
this earth would already become the hoped-for
heaven.

John Wallis
(1651–1717)
St Bartholomew's Church, Oxfordshire

That Learning and Good Sense,
Which rendered him fit for any Publick Station
Induced Him to Choose
A Private Life.

Sergeant J.L. Nyman
(1921–41)

There is no darkness
in all the world
to put out the light
of one small candle

Aircraftsman G.C.E. Hodges
(1902–44)

To live in the hearts
of those we love
is not to die.

Oliver Pell
(1825–91)
St Peter, Wilburton

A Famous Cricketer
An Honest Politician
A Resolute Magistrate

Thomas Bosvile
(1670–1718)
St Andrew, Ufford

~

He chose without these sacred walls to lie
Still here to preach Humility.
The soul that takes her rise from humblest ground
Is always with the highest glory crown'd
If thou woul'st raise thy lofty Towers on high,
Lay thy foundations in Humility:
The Building's strongest and will soonest touch the
sky.

Wing Commander H.J. Fish
(1915–45)
Brookwood Military Cemetery, Surrey

~

To the world
He was just a part
To me he was the world

Lady O'Looney
(died 1870s)

~

Here lies the body of
LADY O'LOONEY
Great niece of BURKE
Commonly called the Sublime
She was Bland, Passionate
and deeply Religious, also
she painted in water colours
and sent several pictures
to the Exhibition
She was first Cousin to
LADY JONES
and of such is the
Kingdom of Heaven.

Radclyffe Hall
(1883–1943)

~

And, if God choose
I shall but love thee better
after death,
Una.

Anne and Arabella Pemberton
(1761 and 1762–1838)

~

This tablet is inscribed to Anne and Arabella
    Pemberton
who in offices of kindness and benevolence
to their poorer neighbours
and uninterrupted sisterly affection for each other
passed their lives
in this their birthplace
and died here
not divided in their deaths
on 27th January 1838.

John and Jane Blacknall
(died 1625)
Abingdon, Oxfordshire

～

When once they liv'd on earth one bed did hold
Their bodies which one minute turn'd to mould.
Being dead, one grave is trusted with that prize
Until the trump doth sound and all must rise.
Here death's stroke even did not part this pair
But by this stroke they more united were.
And what left they behind you plainly see
One only daughter and their charity.
What though the first by death's command did
　　leave us
The second we are sure will never deceive us.

Mary Madden
(1803–30)

~

Sacred to the memory of
Mary
The lovely and beloved wife of
Frederic Madden Esqre.
of the British Museum,
and daughter of Robert Hayton Esqre.
of Sunderland in the County of Durham
Born June 7th 1803.
After an inviolable attachment of ten years duration
unshaken by the united obstacles of fortune and
    prejudice
she was married in this church
April 18th 1829,
and when ten short months had passed away
in the enjoyment of all that youth and beauty can
    bestow,
and in the anticipation of every happiness a fond
    heart can throb for,
to the inexpressible grief and horror of all who loved
    her
she expired
on the 26th February 1830,

having previously given birth the 21st inst. to an
    infant son
Frederick Hayton,
who survived his lamented mother only five days,
and lies by her side in the vaults beneath.
In remembrance of
her loveliness affection and virtue
her afflicted husband erects this monument
as the only means now left in his power
of testifying his lasting sorrow and regrets
She who was
To me the light, the breath of life is gone!
And memory now is as the faded flower
Whose lingering fragrance just recalls how sweet,
How beautiful it has been!

George Pickering
(1574–1645)
Spelsbury, Oxfordshire

∽

Not to prophane (by a Rude Touch)
the dust of his great Masters,
doe we boldly thrust
this aged servant's bones:
whose humble love
an innocent ambition did move;
by creeping near their tombs adored side
to show his body,
not his duty died.

Roger Peachey
(1620–83)

∽

Vicar of Isleham more than 37 years
Buried on Feb 2 1683
to ye great grief of his relations
and the whole Neighbourhood

having been very useful for Physic
as well as Divinity;
he had 10 sons and 8 daughters by one wife.
The eldest son of Grays Inn
was barbarously murdered by Mr Hatton of ye same
    society.
14 other Sons and Daughters
are buried near this place and in the chancel.

They all with him wait for the redemption of their
    bodies.

David Wall
(1739–96)
Ashore, Derbyshire

~

To the Memory of
DAVID WALL
whose superior performance on the
bassoon endeared him to an
extensive musical acquaintance.
His social life closed on the
4th Dec., 1796, in his 57th year.

Maggie
(1940s)
Army mule in France

~

In memory of
MAGGIE
who in her time kicked
Two colonels,
Four majors,
Ten captains,
Twenty-four lieutenants,
Forty-two sergeants,
Four hundred and thirty-two other ranks
AND
One Mills Bomb.

Anne Loder
(died 1714)
Thame, Oxfordshire

~

Farewell awhile thou joy & half my Life
Thou tenderest mother & thou dearest Wife

Olivia Susan Clemens
(1866–1890)
Daughter of Mark Twain

~

Warm summer sun, shine kindly here;
Warm southern wind, blow softly here;
Green sod above, lie light, lie light –
Good-night, dear heart, good-night, good-night.

Anne Chamberlayne
(1667–1692)

~

In a vault, near this place, lies the body of
ANNE, the only daughter of
EDWARD CHAMBERLAYNE, LLD.
Born in London, January 20, 1667,
Who,
For a considerable time, declined the matrimonial
    state,
And scheming many things
Superior to her sex and age,
On the 30th of June 1690,
And under the command of her brother,
With the arms and in the dress of a man,
She approved herself a true VIRAGO,
by fighting undaunted in a fire ship against the
    French,
Upwards of six hours.
She might have given us a race of heroes,
Had not premature fate interposed.
She returned safe from that naval engagement,
And was married, in some months after, to
JOHN SPRAGGE, Esq.
With whom she lived half a year extremely happy,

But being delivered of a daughter, she died
A few days after,
October 30, 1692.

This monument, to his dear and affectionate wife,
    was
erected by her most disconsolate husband.

James Henry Leigh Hunt
(1784–1859)

~

"Write me as one
That loves his fellow men."

Sir Edwin Landseer
(1802–73)

~

He hath made every thing beautiful in his time.

Ernest Courtenay Carter and Lilian Carter
(died 15 April, 1912)
St Mary the Virgin, Longcot

∼

Who after 14 years of self sacrifice in the
cause of Religion and Humanity in this parish
met death when the SS Titanic foundered in
the Atlantic after collision with an Iceberg.

She refusing to leave him when offered a
place in a boat.

The cheerful welcome they gave to all fellow
workers and their keen interest in
everything affecting the public good
will be helpful to and affectionately
remembered by all who knew them.

Douglas, 1st Earl Haig
(1861–1928)

∼

He trusted in God
And tried to do the right.

Margaret Chettle
(1732–1813)

~

This keeps alive the worthy fame of
Margaret Chettle, maiden lady,
who educated the youth of her sex
for forty years at Ripon in useful learning and
adorned them with her virtues.
Free from the gloss of wealth or ostentation,
heaven graced her humble walk in life
with majesty of mind and look,
and acts of pure benevolence,
for though her scanty means
sprung only from her own industry
she made them flow with silent sweetness
to help the work of charity.
Died 1813 aged 81
Merit claimed this tribute to her memory
from her surviving friend,
John Coates,
solicitor of this town.

Henry Page
(1648–1719)
Assumption of the Blessed Virgin Mary, Harlton

∽

All you Good People
that here pass by
as you are now so
once was I, as I am
now so Shall you be
therefore Prepare
to Follow me.

Constance Holben
(died 1947)
St Peter, Barton

∽

With the sun and the skies and the birds above me.

May Whitty and Ben Webster
(1865–1948 and 1864–1947)
Husband and wife actors

~

They were lovely and pleasant in their lives
and in their death they were not divided.

Hester
(19th century)

~

In loving memory of my beloved wife, Hester, the
mother of Edward, Richard, Mary, Penelope, John,
Henry, Michael, Susan, Emily, Charlotte, Amelia,
George, Hugh, Hester, Christopher and Daniel. She
was a great breeder of pugs, a devoted mother and a
dear friend.

Fido
(died 1800s)

~

To the memory of
SIGNOR FIDO
An Italian of Good extraction,
Who came into England,
Not to bite us, like most of his countrymen,
But to gain an honest livelihood.
He hunted not after fame,
Yet acquired it.
Regardless of the praise of his friends,
But most sensible of their love.
Tho' he lived among the great,
He neither learnt nor flattered any vice.
He was no bigot,
tho' he doubted of none of the thirty-nine articles:
And if to follow nature,
And to respect the laws of society
Be philosophy,
He was a perfect philosopher,
A faithful friend,
An agreeable companion,
A loving husband,
And, though an Italian,

Was distinguished by a numerous offspring,
All which he lived to see take good courses.
In his old age he retired
To the house of a clergyman in the country,
Where he finished his earthly race.
And died an honour and an example to the
whole species.
Reader,
This stone is guiltless of flattery;
For he, to whom it was incrib'd
Was not a man,
But a – GREYHOUND.

Olive Gilbert
(1898–1981)
Sang with Ivor Novello

~

In loving and grateful memory
OLIVE GILBERT
1898–1981
We'll gather lilacs again

Rev. Thomas Leman
(died 1826)

～

Sacred to the memory
of the Rev Thomas Leman, of Wenhaston Hall
in this parish,
who died on the 17th day of March 1826;
the last male descendant of his ancient name.
He added to the feelings of a Gentleman,
Talents and Learning without Ostentation,
and Christian Piety without Austerity.
In a curious line of antiquarian research
(The knowledge of Roman Remains in Britain),
he had few superiors;
but in the nobler and more amiable merit
of domestic life
as a husband, a son, a brother, a friend and a master,
he was never exceeded.

Copenhagen
(1808–36)

Here lies
Copenhagen
The charger ridden by
The Duke of Wellington
The entire day, at the
Battle of Waterloo

Born 1808 Died 1836

God's humbler instrument, though meaner clay,
Should share the glory of that glorious day.

John and Mary Palmer
(1600–61 and 1610–60)

~

Here lies John Palmer and Mary his wife
Prisoners of hope to Eternal Life
Who deceased
He May the 15, 1661, aged 61
Mary make room,
To thee I come
And my last home
To the day of doom
Then shall we wake rise live for ay
With Christ a never dying day
Come then my dear we'll sleep in bliss
And in the dust each other kiss
Twice sixteen years we lived together
In sunshine and in stormy weather
In wedlock bands husband and wife
In joy love peace void of all strife
And ten times changed our habitation
And here at last we find our station
When after ten years spent we have
Obtained at length a quiet grave.
She October the 13, 1660, aged 50
I went before

To open death's door
I could not stay
But now give way

Palmers on earth are pilgrims such as I
My pilgrimage is done and here I lye.

Lord Thomson of Fleet
(1894–1976)
Owner "Times Newspapers"

~

He gave a new direction to the British newspaper
industry. A strange and adventurous man from
nowhere,
ennobled by the great virtues of courage and integrity
and faithfulness.

John Brown
(1826–83)

~

This stone
is erected in affectionate remembrance of
John Brown,
the devoted and faithful personal attendant and
beloved friend of Queen Victoria . . . "That friend on
whose fidelity you count, that friend given you by
circumstances over which you have no control, was
God's own gift."

Margaret Pennefather
(died 1880)

~

"With Christ, which is far better."

1st Duke and Duchess of Newcastle
(1592–1676 and 1623–73)

~

Here Lies the Loyal Duke of Newcastle and his
Duchess his second wife by whom he had no issue her
name was Margaret Lucas youngest sister to the Lord
Lucas of Colchester a noble family for all the
Brothers were Valiant and all the Sisters virtuous.
This Duchess was a wise witty & learned Lady, which
her many books do testify she was a most Virtuous &
a loving and careful wife & was with her Lord all
the time of his banishment & miseries & when he
came
home never parted from him in his solitary
retirements.

Howard Ashman
(died 1991)

~

O, That he had one more song to sing.

Mary Atkinson
(1709–86)

~

Periwinkles! Periwinkles!
Was ever her cry;
she laboured to live
Poor and honest to die.
At the last day again
How her old eyes will twinkle;
For no more will she cry
Periwinkle! Periwinkle!

Anna Rhodes
(1764–96)

~

Erected by a sister in memory of her beloved Anna
    Cecilia
of Chatham in the County of Kent.
She departed this Life, June 2d, 1796 aged 32.
Her remains were deposited in the 42d vault in this
    Chapel.

Distinguished by a fine Understanding
and a most amiable Disposition of Heart,
She was the Delight of her Parents,
and the Admiration of all who knew her.
At the Age of 17, the small-pox stripped off all the
    Bloom of youthful Beauty,
And being followed by a dreadful Nervous-disorder,
withered those Prospects of earthly Happiness
which were expected from her uncommon Affection,
    Sensibility and
Tenderness.
After suffering this afflictive Dispensation for many
    Years,
when it was difficult to say which exceeded,
her Sufferings or her Submission;
Her Friends concern for her Sorrows
or their Admiration of her Patience;
She was released by Death
and received into that World where there shall be no
    more Pain
But GOD himself shall wipe away
tears from every eye.

John James
(died 1707)

~

An upright downright honest man.

Samuel Ally
(1804–22)
Kirk Braddan, Isle of Man

~

SAMUEL ALLY
An African and native of St Helena
Died the 28th of may 1822 aged 18 years
Born a slave and exposed
in early life to the corrupt influence
of that unhappy state, he became
A model of TRUTH and PROBITY, for
The more fortunate of any country
or condition
This stone is erected by a grateful
Master, to the memory of a faithful
Servant who repaid the boon of
Liberty with unbounded attachment

Edward Wyndham Tennant
(1897–1916)

"When things were at their worst he would go up and down in the trenches cheering the men, when danger was greatest his smile was loveliest."

In proud and unfading memory of
Edward Wyndham Tennant
4th Batt. Grenadier Guards, eldest son of Lord and Lady Glenconner, who passed to the fuller life in the battle of the Somme 22nd September 1916. Aged 19 years.

He gave his earthly life to such matter as he set great store by: the honour of his country and his home.

John Antell
(died 1878)

~

He was a man of considerable
local reputation as a self-made
scholar, having acquired a varied
knowledge of languages, literature
and science by unaided study &
in the face of many untoward
circumstances.

Mrs Jane Molony
(1765–1839)

~

Sacred to the memory of
Mrs Jane Molony
She died in London in January 1839
She was hot, passionate and tender
And a highly accomplished lady and a superb drawer
in water colour which was much admired in the
exhibition rooms in

Somerset House some years past
"Though lost for ever, yet a friend is dear,
The heart yet pays a tributary tear"

Bryan Tunstall
(died 1790)

Here lies poor but honest
Bryan Tunstall.
He was a most expert Angler,
until Death, envious of his merit,
threw out his line, hooked him
and landed him here the 21st day of April
1790

William Battle
(1791–1860)
St Mary, Swaffham Bulbeck

For upward of 40 years the faithful servant of John
   King
of Bottisham who erected this stone to perpetuate the
deep sense he entertained of his worth and integrity.

Weep not for me but be content
I was not yours but only lent
Wipe off those tears and weep no more
I am not lost but gone before.

Anne de Gaulle
(1928–1948)
Mentally-handicapped daughter of Charles de Gaulle

"Now she is like all the others"

Jack Williams
(19th century)

~

Here lies Jack Williams. He done his damnedest.

Boatswain
(1803–8)
Dog of Lord Byron

~

Near this spot
are deposited the remains of one
who possessed Beauty without Vanity,
Strength without Insolence,
Courage without Ferocity,
and all the Virtues of Man without his Vices.
This praise, which would be unmeaning Flattery,
if inscribed over human Ashes,
is but a just Tribute to the memory of
Boatswain, a DOG
who was born in Newfoundland, May 1803,
and died at Newstead, Nov 18, 1808.

Captain William Bligh
(1753–1817)

~

Sacred
to the memory of
William Bligh, Esquire, FRS
Vice Admiral of the Blue,
The celebrated navigator
who first transplanted the bread fruit tree
from Otaheite to the West Indies,
Bravely fought the battles of his country,
and died beloved, respected and lamented,
on the 7th day of December 1817.

Elizabeth Corbett
(died 1724)

~

Here rests a woman good without pretence,
Blest with plain Reason & with sober Sense;
No Conquests she but or'e her Self, desired,
No Arts essayed but not to be admired

Passion and Pride were to her Soul unknown,
Convinced that Virtue only is our own.
So Unaffected, so composed a Mind;
So firm, yet soft: so strong, yet so refined,
Heaven as its purest Gold by Tortures tried
The Saint sustained it but the Woman died.

Sir William Dyer
(died 1641)

~

My dearest dust, could not thy hasty day
Afford thy drowsy patience leave to stay
One hour longer: so that we might either
Sit up or go to bed together?
But since thy finished labour hath possessed
Thy weary limbs with early rest,
Enjoy it sweetly: and thy widow bride
Shall soon repose her by thy slumbering side.
Whose business, now, is only to prepare
My nightly dress and call to prayer:
Mine eyes wax heavy and the day grows old.
The dew falls thick, my blood grows cold.
Draw, draw the closed curtains: and make room:
My dear, my dearest dust; I come, I come.

Dorothy Carlotta Brownlow
(1907–66)

In
gratitude to GOD
and in ever loving memory of
Dorothy CARLOTTA
deeply loved wife of
PEREGRINE LORD BROWNLOW.
She sleeps in peace in the deep blue Jamaican Sea

A BIRD with a broken wing
A CHILD with a crippled limb
A MAN with a wounded body
A GIRL with an aching heart

They were her especial children
whom she loved and of such is
the Kingdom of Heaven.

Thomas Cotes
(died 1648)
Wing Parish Church, Buckinghamshire

∼

Honest old Thomas Cotes, that sometime was
Porter at Ascott-hall, hath now (alas)
Left his key, lodge, fire, friends and all to have
a room in heaven, this is that good man's grave.
Reader, prepare for thine, for none can tell
But that you two may meet tonight, farewell.

Edward and Mabel Courtenay
(died 1419)

∼

What wee gave, wee have;
What wee spent, wee had;
What we left, we lost.

William Ewart
(1763–1823)
St James's, Liverpool

~

To the memory
of William Ewart
An intelligent, indefatigable
and successful
merchant
A virtuous and amiable
man.
His widow and children
with the deepest feeling
of reverence and regret
have raised this monument.

Sir Noel Coward
(1899–1973)

~

A talent to amuse.

Sir Maurice Bowra
(1898–1971)

～

Send us to Hell or Heaven or where you will,
Promise us only, you'll be with us still:
Heaven, without you, would be too dull to bear,
And Hell will not be Hell if you are there.

Richard and Mary Chambers
(died 1770 and 1772)
St Mary the Virgin, Orton Waterville

～

Thro' Life they passed
Virtue their constant Guide
Happy they lived
And as they lived, they died.

Richard Austin
(18th century)
Blacksmith

My Sledge and Hammer lye declined,
My bellows too have lost their wind,
My Fire's extinct, my Forge decayed
And in the dust my Vice is laid.
My Coal is spent, my Iron's gone,
My nail's are drove, my Work is done.

Robert Logie
(18th century)
Carpenter

He was a just and pious
man and to say more is un
necessary and to say less
would be ungrateful

Mary Palmer
(1736–95)
St Mary, Brampton

~

If Modest Worth with Gentle Manners crowned
And every opening Virtue smiling round
Could save the friend of Humankind from Fate
Or shield from Death whate'er was Good and Great
This Weeping Marble had not ask'd thy Tear
Or sadly told Fair Excellence lies here.

Katherine Chapman
(1780–1802)
St Mary, St Neots

~

If e'er soft sorrow from thy Breast did flow
If e'er thy Bosom felt another's woe
If e'er an Object to thy Heart was dear
Bloomed to thy wish, and to thy soul was near,
This plaintive Stone may claim of thee a Tear
A Tear of joy and hope in Heav'n above
The World of Friendship, Harmony and Love.

John Baylie
(1732–77)

~

Asleep beneath this humble Stone,
Lies honest, harmless, simple John:
Who free from Guilt & Care & Strife,
Here cloud's his inoffensive Life,
His worth was great, his failings few,
He practised all the good he knew.
And did no harm, his only Sin
Was that he loved a drop of Gin;
And when his favourite was not near
contented took his horn of Beer:
Tho' weak his head, to make amends
Heaven gave him health, content & Friends.
This little Village Nursed and Bred him,
'Twas there he Lived, Caressed by all,
The favourite of the Servant's Hall,
With them he ate his daily Bread:
They loved him Living, mourn him Dead.
And now have kindly Joined to Raise
This little Tombstone to his praise,
Nor should the learned and the wise
such humble merit ever Despise;
Who knows but John may find a place

Where wit must never show its face.
Farewell John. Grant Heaven that we
Harmless may live and die like thee.

Edith Cavell
(1865–1915)
Shot by Germans for helping allied prisoners escape

~

Edith Cavell
Brussels
Dawn
October 12th
1915

Patriotism is not enough
I must have no hatred or
bitterness for anyone.

Mary Beach
(1647–1725)

~

To the Memory of
Mary Beach
Who died Nov 5 1725 Aged 78

Alex Pope, whom she nursed in
his infancy and constantly
attended for thirty eight years
in
Gratitude to a faithful old servant,
Erected this stone.

Charles Ward
(1707–70)

~

A dutiful son, a loving brother, and an affectionate
husband.

N.B. This stone was not erected by Susan his wife.
She erected a stone to John Salter her second
husband, forgetting the affection of Charles Ward.

John Anstey
(1757–1819)
St Mary, Trumpington
~

To the memory of
A tender husband
A most anxious and affectionate father
A friend beloved
For his unassuming virtues
A poet admired
For his elegant wit and inoffensive satire
For his polite acquirements and sound judgement
And classical taste
This tablet
Is inscribed by his afflicted wife
and grateful children.

George Cruikshank
(1792–1878)

~

In loving memory
of
George Cruikshank
Artist
Designer, etcher, painter

For 30 years a total abstainer
and ardent pioneer and champion
by pencil, word and pen,
of universal abstinence
from intoxicating drinks . . .
This monument is erected
by his affectionate widow
Eliza Cruikshank.

Zak Johnson
(1975–86)

~

ZAK

JOHNSON
Springer Spaniel
died March 12th 1986
aged 11 years
The pleasure was all ours

Dorothy
Richard
Charlotte.

Charles A. Lindbergh
(1902–74)

~

If I take wings of the morning, and dwell
in the uttermost parts of the sea.

Chapter 2

UNTIMELY DEATHS

Some of the most poignant epitaphs are those composed by parents whose children died before them, and the sentimentality of this form of tribute reached its peak during the Victorian period. But all forms of untimely death, even when self-inflicted, brought with them a powerful range of sentiments and give rise to an immensely varied selection of epitaphs.

Revd Dr Martin Luther King Jr
(1929–68)

~

Free at Last, Free at Last
Thank god Almighty
I'm Free at Last.

Tho. Welsted
(1658–76)
Old Cloisters, Winchester College

~

Beneath this Marble is Buried
Tho. Welsted
Who was Struck Down by the Throwing of a Stone.
He was First in this School
And we Hope is not last in Heaven
Whither he went
Instead of to Oxford.
January 13, 1676
Aged 18.

The eldest son of Ben Jonson
(16th century)

~

Farewell, thou child of my right hand and joy;
My sin was too much hope of thee, lov'd boy,
Seven years thou wert lent to me and I thee pay
Exacted by thy fate on the just day.
O, could I lose all father, now. For why
Will man lament the state he should envy?
To have so soon scap'd World's and flesh's rage,
And, if no other misery, yet age?
Rest in soft peace and ask'd say here doth lie
Ben Jonson his best piece of poetrie.
For whose sake, henceforth, all his vows be such
As what he loves may never live too much.

Unknown
(died 1776)
Bampton, Devon

~

By my i i i i
Here he lies
In a sad pickle
Kill'd by icicle
1776

2nd British Division
(1944)
Kohima War Cemetery, Assam, India

~

When you go home
Tell them of us and say
for your tomorrow
We gave our today

Unknown
(19th century)
Seattle, Washington

~

Beneath this stone our baby lies.
It neither cries nor hollers.
It lived but one and twenty days
And cost us ninety dollars.

Sir Robert Shirley
(1629-56)
*Royalist beheaded by Cromwell for building Staunton
Harold Church, Leicestershire*

~

In the year 1653
when all things Sacred were throughout the nation
Either demollisht or profaned
Sir Robert Shirley, Barronet
Founded this Church
whose singular praise it is
to have done the best things in the worst times

And
hoped them in the most calamitous.
The righteous shall be had in everlasting remembrance.

Ann Sims
(1769–84)

~

As blossoms in the early Spring
Do wither and decay:
So God cut off her youthful days
And took her life away.

Hannah Twynoy
(1670–1703)
Eaten by a tiger that had escaped from the circus

IN MEMORY OF
HANNAH TWYNOY
Who died October 23rd 1703
Aged 33 Years.

In bloom of Life
She's snatched from hence,
She had not room
To make defence;
For Tyger fierce
Took life away.
And here she lies
In a bed of Clay,
Until the Resurrection Day.

George Warburton
(died 1850)
San Francisco

Here lies the body of George Warburton
late of Guildford, England,
who died 23 October 1850
by the explosion of his own pistol.
It was not one of the modern sort
but an old-fashioned breech-loader
with the barrel bound in brass wire.
And of such is the kingdom of Heaven.

Mary Ann South
(1825–95)
Ayot St Lawrence, Herts
George Bernard Shaw, when asked why he had decided to
live in the village, declared that if 70 years was considered
a short life there then it must be a good place to live.

HER TIME WAS SHORT

Bridgett Applethwait
(1693–1737)

~

Beneath the remains of her Brother Edward
And of her Husband Arthur
Here lies the Body of Bridgett Applethwait
Once Bridgett Nelson.
After the Fatigues of a Married Life,
Borne by her with Incredible Patience,
For four years and three Quarter, bating three weeks;
And after the Enjoyment of the Glorious Freedom
Of an Easy and Unblemisht Widowhood
For four years and upwards
She resolved to run the Risk of a second Marriage-
    Bed
But death forbad the Banns
And having with an apoplectic Dart,
(The same instrument with which he had Formerly
Dispatch't her Mother)
Touch't the most Vital part of her Brain;
She must have fallen Directly to the ground
(as one Thunder-strook)
If she had not been Catch'd and Supported
by her intended Husband,
Of which Invisible Bruise,

After a long struggle of some Sixty Hours,
With that Grand Enemy to Life,
But the certain and Merciful Friend to
Helpless Old Age
In Terrible Convulsion, Plaintive Groans
Or stupefying sleep
Without recovery of her speech or senses,
She dyed on the 12th day of Sept in the Year
Of our Lord 1737 and of her own Age 44.

Richard Wallis
(1744–67)
All Saints, Longstanton

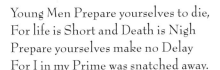

Young Men Prepare yourselves to die,
For life is Short and Death is Nigh
Prepare yourselves make no Delay
For I in my Prime was snatched away.

A Maid of Queen Elizabeth
(17th century)

~

Here lies, the Lord have mercy upon her,
One of her Majesty's maids of honour:
She was both young, slender and pretty,
She died a maid, the more the pity.

Hannah Rogers and four of her children
(1801–36)
St George, Littleport

~

Lo! here I lie by my dear babes
All covered with cold clay
Hoping with joy to meet my Lord
At the resurrection day.

Michael Kennedy
(1842–78)

~

Erected
by the
Parliament of Victoria
to the
memory of
POLICE-SERGEANT
MICHAEL KENNEDY,
Native of West Meath, Ireland,
Aged 36 years,
who was
CRUELLY MURDERED BY CRIMINALS
in the wombat ranges near Mansfield
on the 26th October 1878.
He died in the service of his country
of which he was an ornament,
highly respected by all good citizens, and
a terror to evil-doers . . .

Unknown soldier
(Armistice Day 1920)
Westminster Abbey

~

Beneath this stone rests the body
Of a British warrior
Unknown by name or rank
Brought from France to lie among
The most illustrious of the land
And buried here on Armistice Day
11 Nov: 1920, in the presence of
His Majesty King George V
His Ministers of State
The Chiefs of his Forces
And a vast concourse of the Nation.

Thus are commemorated the many
Multitudes who during the Great
War of 1914–1918 gave the most that
Man can give life itself
For God
For King and Country
For loved ones home and empire
For the sacred cause of justice and
The freedom of the world.

They buried him among the kings because he
had done good toward God and toward
his house.

John Chapman, William Goosey, Charles Favel
(died 1878)
St Andrew, Great Staughton

~

In the belfrey of this church
John Chapman aged 40
William Goosey aged 15
Charles Favel aged 11
were instantaneously killed by a flash of lightning
on 17th July 1787
about 4 in the afternoon
in the presence of several persons
whose lives were miraculously preserved.

This stone is erected at the expense of the Parish
to perpetuate the Memory of that awful catastrophe.

Whilst o'er their grave the tears of pity flow
May public virtue spring from private woe.
Warned by their fate, the careless and secure
Shall learn tho' life's uncertain death is sure.

Mary Richards
(1740-71)
St Mary, Doddington

～

All ye who stop to read this stone
Consider how soon she was gone.
Death doth not always warning give
Therefore be careful how you live.

William Beamish, George Crow, Isaac Harley, Thomas South
(died 1816)
St Mary, Ely

~

Here lye interred in one grave the Bodies of
William Beamish
George Crow
John Dennis
Isaac Harley
and
Thomas South

Who were all executed at Ely on the 28th day of June
1816,
Having been convicted at the Special Assizes holden
there
of divers Robberies during the Riots at Ely and
Littleport
in the month of May in that year.

May their awful Fate
Be a warning to others.

Mary Ann Weems
(died May 1819)
St Mary, Godmanchester

~

As a Warning
To the Young of both Sexes

This stone is erected by public subscription
Over the remains of Mary Ann Weems
Who at an early age became acquainted
with Thomas Weems formerly of this Parish
this connection terminating in a compulsory
Marriage occasioned him first to desert her
and wishing to be married to another Woman
he filled up the measure of his iniquity
by resolving to murder his Wife
which he barbarously perpetrated at Wendy
on their Journey towards London towards which place
he had induced her to go under the mask
of reconciliation May the 7th 1819.
He was taken within a few hours after
the crime was committed, tried and
subsequently executed at Cambridge
on the 7th of August in the Same Year.

Ere Crime you perpetrate survey this Stone
Learn hence the God of Justice sleeps not on his
     Throne
But marks the sinner with unerring eye
The suffering Victim hears and makes the Guilty die

Donald Robertson
(1722-85)
Northmaven, Shetland

~

He was a peaceable quiet man & to all appearance a sincere Christian. His death was very much regretted, which was caused by the stupidity of Laurence Tulloch of Clotherton who sold him nitre instead of Epsom salts by which he was killed in the space of 3 hours after taking a dose of it.

Charles Eyre
(1860–69)

~

This marble is sacred to the memory of Chas. Eyre a
youth of great promise who an only son was
deservedly beloved by his parents to wit Geo &
Marguerite Eyre. A too early fate snatched him
out of this life when not born quite 10 years. He was
one of the students in the college of Boulogne-sur-
mer in France where he eminently distinguished
himself in his studies & endeared himself to his
fellow colleagues.

He died the 8th of the month of Jan 1869
oppressed by a deadly fever. His relics not his soul are
buried in the vault of Chas Eyre his ancestor, outside
this Church. Charlie is not dead: the darling is now
gone to school where he will learn forever goodness.
Jesus himself is his father, brother & best guide.
Christ rules the blessed in heaven by love alone in
that tranquil region the ever dear one lives: the
guardian angel holds his tender hands.

Death has not taken him: he whom we say is
snatched away by gloomy fate, still lives, ever
freed from pollution stain.

The principal of the college has declared that Charlie has left at the college the remembrance of a beautiful intelligence & Excellent heart. The principal wished & Advised that the memory of a youth so excellent & ingenuous & his intelligence should be especially kept in remembrance. The weeping heavily distracted father has taken care that this monument should be erected.

Charlie was born 24th Jan 1859 died of typhus fever & he learned to speak French in 7 months, fluently: he possessed a noble mind and loved truthfulness indeed his father ever abominating guile, taught him sincerity. He intended, God willing, when he had finished his education in France that he should consecutively enter universities in Germany & Italy & then if he pleased should take a degree in an English university, but alas his father's hopes have been suddenly blasted: this affliction is as appalling as any ever recorded. By universal law, death is decreed: but the time may be stayed by the intercessory prayer of parents; but here that was wanting.

John Johnston
(1796–1829)
St Wendreda, March

Sacred to the memory of the late John Johnston Gent
    whose death
was occasioned by the accidental discharge of his gun.

In grateful recognition
Of his good humour and amiable disposition
The Members of the Doddington Hunt
Of which he was a staunch supporter
In conjunction with a few private friends
Have erected this small tablet
As their sad remembrance of
The Melancholy event

Flora Stewart
(1864–95)
St Martin, Little Stukeley

~

This tablet is erected by many friends in memory of
Flora Lucy Stewart,
eldest daughter of the Rev. James Stewart of this
    Parish.
Having laboured diligently in the service of her
    Divine Master
first in her father's parish
and afterwards as a missionary to the Chinese
    Women at Ku-Chang,
she met her death at Hwasang
in the massacre of the English missionaries
August 1895.

Eric Liddle
(1902–45)
Runner and missionary.
Died of a brain tumour in a Japanese internment camp
at Weifang, China

~

They shall mount up with wings as eagles
They shall run, and not be weary.

J.W. Nightall
(died June 1944)

~

This tablet commemorates the heroic action of
  Fireman J.C. Nightall
who gave his life and Driver B. Gimers who was badly
  injured
whilst detaching a blazing wagon from an
  ammunition train
at Soham Station at 1.43 am on June 2nd 1944.

The station was totally destroyed
and considerable damage was done by the explosion.

The devotion of these brave men saved the town of
   Soham
from grave destruction.
Signalman Bridges was killed on duty
and Guard H. Clark suffered from shock.

Be strong and quit yourselves like men.

Catherine Alsopp
(hanged herself 1905)
Sheffield

~

Here lies a poor woman who always was tired,
For she lived in a place where help wasn't hired,
Her last words on earth were, "Dear friends, I am
   going,
Where washing ain't done nor cooking nor sewing,
And everything there is exact to my wishes,
For there they don't eat, there's no washing of dishes,
I'll be where loud anthems will always be ringing
(But having no voice, I'll be out of the singing).
Don't mourn for me now, don't grieve for me never,
For I'm going to do nothing for ever and ever."

Sir Charles Rose
(died 1913)

~

From the effects of an aeroplane flight.

Piers Gaveston
(died 1312)

~

In the Hollow of this Rock
Was beheaded,
On the 17th day of July, 1312,
By Barons lawless as himself,
PIERS GAVESTON, Earl of Cornwall;
the minion of a hateful King:
In Life and Death,
A memorable instance of Misrule.

Mary, Sarah and Eliza Atwood
(1794–1808, 1801–8 and 1803–8)

~

Mary, Sarah and Eliza Atwood who were poisoned by
eating fungous vegetables mistaken for champignons
on the 11th day of October 1808
and died at the ages of 14, 7 and 5 years
within a few hours of each other
in excruciating circumstances.
The father, mother and now, alas, an only child,
partakers of the same meal,
have survived with debilitated
constitutions and to lament so dreadful a calumny.
This monument is erected to perpetuate the fatal
events as an awful caution to others, let it be too
a solemn warning that in our most grateful
enjoyments even in our necessary food
may lurk deadly poison.

Lionel and Dorothy Alington
(died 1638)
Holy Trinity, Bottisham

Stay Passenger and wonder whom these stones
Had learned to speak two infant Alingtons
These the world's strangers come not here to dwell
They tasted, liked it not, and bad farewell.
Nature hath granted what they begged with tears
As soon as they begun to end their years.

Rt Hon. William Huskisson
(1770–1830)
One of the first people to be killed in a railway accident

For ten years the representative of this city in
    Parliament.
This station he relinquished in MDCCCXXIII,
When yielding to a sense of publick duty
He accepted the offer of being returned for
Liverpool.

His death was occasioned by an accident near that
   town
On the XV of September MDCCCXXX
And changed a scene of triumphant rejoicing
into one of general mourning.
At the urgent solicitation of his constituents
He was interred in the cemetery there
amid the unaffected sorrow of all classes of people.

Edwin Calvert
(1842–59)

~

In memory of Edwin Calvert, son of Richard Calvert,
of Skipton, known by the title of "Commander in
Chief." He was the smallest and most perfect human
being in the world, being under 36 inches in height,
and weighing 25 lb. He died much lamented and
deeply regretted by all who knew him,
August 7th 1859, aged 17 years.

Alice and Jane Balam
(1632–58 and 1638–58)
St Mary, Sawston

~

Virgins' ashes sleep securely,
Here's no Sin, nor Shame to fright them
Their bright Lamp did shine too purely
For Death's Shadows to benight them.
Holy Raptures feed their slumbers
With delight too high for numbers.

These Souls, too rich a Prize for mortal Race
Endowed with Nature and the Gift of Grace
Once viewed this World and then in much disdain
Left this void World in Glory now to raigne.

Gordon Hamilton-Fairley
(1930–75)
Killed by an IRA bomb

~

First Professor Clinical Oncology
Killed by a terrorist bomb
It matters not how a man dies but how he lives

Elizabeth Crimpling
(1681–1701)
St Leonard, Leverington

~

A Modest Dutiful
Child lyeth Here
Who was Beloved of
Her Father Dear – he at
her Death did Weep and Moan
& that in her Stead himself
had gone. But now (as
holy David he doth say)
Since Pleased God to call my
Child Away, She shall
No more hither Return to me
I hope to meet in Joy eternally.

Robert Cotton
(1683–97)

~

He was a youth of very great hope,

the vivacity of his wit was wonderful

His questions and answers were discerning, nice and
  pleasant

With all this he was Religious, Compassionate,
  Charitable

Affable with his companions,

meek in his disposition

And yet there were visible in him all the marks of a
  sprightly courage.

He had made a considerable Progress in all the
  knowledge that suited with his years

He was so inquisitive after truth that had Time
  ripened his Perfection

He would have shown himself a worthy offspring of
  the Cotton family

so famed for learning.

While he remained in this world

He was the Joy of his Parents and the Delight of all
  who knew him

Innocent and Beautiful as those Angels

with whom he is now singing of Praises of his

Creator,
God blessed for ever.

General Charles Gordon
(1833–85)
Killed by Mahdi troops besieging Khartoum

He saved an empire by his warlike genius,
he ruled vast provinces with justice, wisdom and
   power.
And lastly obedient to his sovereign's command
He died in the heroic attempt to save men,
Women and children from imminent and deadly
   Peril.

Lady Mary Wortley Montague
(1689–1762)

~

Sacred to the memory of
The Right Honourable
Lady Mary Wortley Montague,
Who happily introduced from Turkey,
into this Country,
The Salutary Art
Of inoculating the Small-Pox.
Convinced of its Efficacy
She first tried it with success
On her own Children;
And then recommended the practice of it
To her fellow-Citizens,
Thus by her Example and Advice,
We have softened the Virulence,
And escaped the danger of this malignant Disease,
To perpetuate the memory of such Benevolence;
And to express her Gratitude
For the benefit She herself has received
From this alleviating Art,
This Monument is erected by
Henrietta Inge
relict of Theodore William Inge Esq.

Mr Partridge
(died 1861)

~

What! Kill a partridge in the month of May!
Was that done like a sportsman? eh, death, eh?

Trooper Edward Gaffney
(died 1961)

~

As the days roll by, this day we do recall.
The noonday sun.
The twittering of strange birds.
The brown meandering stream, that heard the din of
    battle
And carried you to history, to join the brave.
That swords be turned into ploughshares.
Killed in the Congo (Zaire) on the 13th September
    1961

Archibald Campbell Marquess of Argyll
(died 1661)

~

Beheaded near this cathedral A.D. 1661
Leader in council and in field for reformed religion
"I see a Crown on the King's Head
He hastens me to a better
Crown than his own"

Various
(19th century)

~

To the memory of
Two officers
Twenty one sergeants, twenty seven
corporals, nine drummers, four hundred and
thirty nine privates, forty seven women
and twenty one children of the seventy
eighth Highland Regiment, in all amounting
to six hundred and sixty nine, who died on
the banks of the River Indus in Sinde,

between the sixth day of September one
thousand eight hundred and forty four and
the fourth day of March one thousand eight
hundred and forty five.

Susanna Barford
(1687–97)

This world to her was but a traged play,
She came and saw't, dislikt, and pass'd away.

Pfc Cameron
(died 1942)
US Marine

And when he goes to heaven
To Saint Peter he will tell:
Another Marine reporting, sir,
I've served my time in hell!

Name and date unknown

❧

He passed the bobby without any fuss,
And he passed the cart of hay,
He tried to pass a swerving bus,
And then he passed away.

Richard Taylor
(1707–19)
St Peter, Witcham

❧

Master Richard Taylor
only child of
Richard and Dorothy Taylor
Who was cropt by a Fever
When near the 13th year of his Age
Having been while he lived
One of the fairest Flowers
That Time has produced.

Wallace Hartley and others
(died 1912)

~

In memory of
the Devoted Musicians
Wallace Henry Hartley, Bandmaster
John Fredrick Preston Clark
Percy Cornelius Taylor
John Wesley Woodward
W. Theodore Brailey
John Law Hume
Georges Krins
Roger Bricoux
Who were drowned
Still playing
As the Titanic went down
April 15, 1912

W.S. Gilbert
(1836–1911)
Librettist
Died of heart attack after rescuing a girl from drowning

His foe was folly
& his weapon wit

Mary Chowder
(20th century)

Here lies the body of Mary Chowder,
She burst while drinking a Seidlitz Powder;
She couldn't wait till it effervesced,
So now she's gone to eternal rest

Walter Raleigh
(1552–1618)

~

Within the chancel of this church was interred
the body of the
Great Sir Walter Raleigh Kt
On the day he was beheaded
In Old Palace Yard, Westminster
Oct 29th Ano Dom 1618

READER – Should you reflect on his errors
Remember his many virtues
And that he was a mortal

Written the night before execution:
Even such is time that takes in trust
Our youth, our joys, and all we have,
And pays us but with age and dust:
Who in the dark and silent grave
When we have wandered all our ways
Shuts up the story of our days.
And from which earth and grave and dust
The Lord shall raise me up, I trust.

Anne Anstey
(died 1719 aged 4 months)
St Mary, Brinkley

❧

Let no sad Tear these Infant Relicks mourn
A Soul unspotted hence to heaven was born.
From Heaven it came, & gain'd a quick return
A Longer Stay might here have given Delight
But she secur'd her Conquest by her Flight.

Reader, may Innocence thus bless thy Fate
Or pious Grief thy Failings expiate,
And be thy Vict'ry in thy Death compleat!
So shall thy Soul with hers triumphant shine
When Heaven shall wake her pious dust & thine.

Thomas Thatcher
(1742-69)

❧

A grenadier of the Ninth Regiment
of Hants Militia, who died of a
Violent Fever, Contracted by drinking
Small Beer when Hot.

In Grateful Remembrance of
whose Universal
Goodwill Towards his Comrades
This Stone
Is Placed here at Their Expense
As a Small
Testimony of Their Regard and Concern.
Here sleeps in Peace a Hampshire Grenadier,
Who caught his death by drinking cold small beer.
Soldiers, be wise from his untimely fall,
And when you're hot drink strong or not at all.

Anna, Letitia and George
(died 1783)
St Davids, Wales

~

They tasted of life's bitter cup,
Refused to drink their potion up,
But turned their little heads aside
Disgusted with the taste – and died.

William Greenwood
(1786–1820)

~

In memory of William Greenwood of Pecket Well,
who was found dead at Bridgewellhead in Wadsworth
on the 14th day of April 1820.
He was forsaken by a bad wife
who enforced him to serve his Majesty in the
Third York Militia for 8 years.
He left a girl aged 16 years to be becozened
by her mother's father out of his money.
His own father deposed for felony.
His own brother arranged before a magistrate
for his raiment which he had bequeathed to him
before his death in the presence of two witnesses.
His thread of life spun
His age near 35 years.
And in his trouble dropped down dead,
And left this vale of tears.

Captain Anthony Wedgwood
(dates unknown)

~

Sacred to the Memory of
Captain Anthony Wedgwood
Accidentally shot by His Gamekeeper
Whilst out shooting.
"Well done thou good and faithful servant"

Catherine Cranwell
(1763–83)
St Andrew, Abbots Ripton

~

If numbers suffer, e'er they yield their Breath
Severe Affliction in a Ling'ring Death
How bless'd thy Lot? ordained at once to Die
Without a Groan, a Murmur or a Sigh.
Heav'n points ye Lightning at thy Virtuous Breast
And angels waft thee to eternal rest.

Claude du Vall
(1643–70)
Hanged at Tyburn

~

Here lies Du Vall: Reader, if male thou art,
Look to thy Purse, if Female to thy heart.
Much havoc has he made of both, for all
Men he made stand, and women he made fall.

The second conqueror of the Norman race,
Knights to his arms did yield and Ladies to his face,
Old Tyburn's glory; England's illustrious thief,
Du Vall, the Ladies' joy; du Vall, the Ladies' grief.

John Smith
(died 1842)

~

In memory of
John Smith who met
violent death near this spot,
18 hundred 40 too. He was shot
by his own pistol
It was not one of the new kind
but an old-fashioned
brass barrel, and of such is the
Kingdom of Heaven.

Marilyn Monroe
(1926–62)

~

Bust to dust.
Lashes to ashes.

Names unknown
(died 1689)

~

Here two young Danish Soldiers lye
the one in quarrel chanced to die;
The other head by their own Law,
With sword was sever'd at one Blow.

Edward Howell
(died 1852)

~

To the memory
of Edward Howell
who departed this life
November 9 1852
Aged 9 months

Here lies the grief
of a fond mother
and blasted expectations
of an indulgent father.

Sarah Lloyd
(1778–1800)

~

Sarah Lloyd
Suffered a just and
ignominious death
for admitting her
Abandoned seducer
In the dwelling house of her
Mistress on the
3rd of October 1799
& becoming the instrument
In his hands of the crime of
Robbery & Housebreaking.
These were her last words:
May my example be a warning to thousands.

Fanny Robinson
(1844-60)
All Saints, Milton

~

She faded from the sight as flowers
In summer fall – she vanished as the rainbow
After sultry showers – she sank pale and
Like the fleecy snow, which in the sunbeams
Melts – and we have laid her in her peaceful
Resting place to wait the Coming of her Lord.

Peter Heiwood
(died 1640)

~

Peter Heiwood, younger son of Peter Heiwood,
one of the Counsellors of Jamaica,
by Grace, Daughter of Sir John Muddeford,
who apprehended Guy Faux, with his dark Lanthorn.
And for his zealous Prosecution of Papists,
as Justice of the Peace,
was stabbed in Westminster Hall,

by John James, a Dominican Friar,
Anno Dom 1640
Reader, if not a Papist bred,
Upon such Ashes gently tread.

Name unknown
(died 1905)
Sheldon, Vermont

~

Unknown man shot in
The Jennison & Gallup Co's store
while in the act of burglarizing
the safe Oct 13, 1905
(Stone bought with money
found on his person.)

George Johnson
(dates unknown)
Tombstone, Arizona
~

Hanged by mistake

Jerry Howells
(18th century)
~

Death has taken little Jerry
Son of Joseph and Serena Howells.
Seven days did he wrestle with the dysentery
Then he perished in his little bowels.

William and Thomas Bradbury
(died 1832)

Here lie interred the dreadfully
Bruised and lacerated bodies of
William Bradbury and Thomas his son
both of Greenfield who were together
savagely murdered in an unusually
horrid manner on Monday night, April 2, 1832

Such interest did their tragic end excite
That, ere they were removed from human sight,
Thousands on thousands daily came to see
The bloody scene of the catastrophe.

Chapter 3

THE GREAT AND THE GOOD

The great and the famous normally inspire grand epitaphs which seem, to their writers, more adequately to express the gravitas that these momentous beings deserved. Some merit adulation, praise and uncritical adoration — many at great length — while others in this category are simply ordinary people, pursuing a variety of careers, but in a manner that inspired reverence over and above affection.

Sir Christopher Wren
(1632–1723)
St Paul's Cathedral

~

Si monumentum requiris circumspice
(trans: If you want a monument, look around)

Oscar Wilde
(1854–1900)
Pere Lachaise Cemetery, Paris
from "The Ballad of Reading Gaol"

~

And alien tears will fill for him
Pity's long broken urn,
For his mourners will be outcast men,
And outcasts always mourn.

Dame Sybil Thorndike CH
(1882–1976)

~

Saint Joan or Hecuba, great actress of your age,
All womanhood your part, the world your stage.
To each good cause you lent your vigorous tongue,
Swept through the years the champion of the young.
And now the scripts lie fading on the shelf,
We celebrate your finest role – yourself;
The calls, the lights grow dim, but not this part,
The Christian spirit, the great generous heart.

Richard Turner
(1790–1846)
Preston

~

Beneath this stone are deposited the remains of
RICHARD TURNER, author of the word Teetotal as
applied to abstinence from all intoxicating liquors,
who departed this life on the 27th day of October,
1846, aged 56 years.

Theodore, King of Corsica
(died 1756)

~

Near this place is interred
Theodore, King of Corsica;
Who died in this parish, Dec. 11, 1756
immediately after leaving
the King's Bench Prison,
by the benefit of the act of insolvency,
in consequence of which
he registered the Kingdom of Corsica
for the use of his creditors.

The grave, great teacher, to a level brings
heroes and beggars, galley-slaves and kings.
But Theodore this moral lesson learn'd, ere dead;
Fate pour'd its lessons on his living head,
Bestow'd a kingdom, and denied him bread.

Sir Henry Morton Stanley
(1841–1904)
Explorer

~

BULA MATARI

1841–1904

AFRICA
(trans: Breaker of rocks)

Dame Dorothy Selby
(1572–1641)
Traditionally discoverer of the Gunpowder plot

~

She was DORCAS
Whose curious Needle wound th'abused Stage
Of this lewd World into the golden Age
Whose Pen of steel and silken lock enroll'd
The Acts of Jonah in records of Gold
Whose Art disclosed that Plot, which, had it taken,
Rome had triumphed and Britain's walls had shaken.

She was
In heart a Lydia, and in tongue a Hanna,
In Zeale a Ruth, in wedlock a Susanna,
Prudently simple, providently Wary,
To the world a Martha, and to heaven a Mary.

Dylan Thomas
(1914–53)
from his poem "Fern Hill"
~

Time held me green and dying
Though I sang in my chains like the sea . . .

Sir Donald Wolfit
(1902–68)
Actor-manager
~

"Is't not the King? Ay, every inch a King"   *King Lear*
"Well roared, Lion!"   *Midsummer Night's Dream*

George Frederick Handel
(1685–1759)

~

The most excellent
Musician
Any age has produced;
Whose compositions were a
Sentimental Language
Rather than mere Sounds;

And surpassed the Power of
Words in expressing
The various Passions
Of the human heart.

Sir Edward Wynton
(died 1636)
St Mary's Church, Battersea

~

Alone, unarm'd, a tyger he oppress'd,
And crush'd to death the monster of a beast;
Twice twenty mounted Moors he overthrew
Singly on foot; some wounded, some he slew,
Dispers'd the rest. What more could Samson do?

Ivor Novello
(1893–1951)

~

Blaze of lights and music calling, Music weeping,
rising, falling, Like a rare & precious diamond
His brilliance still lives on.

Edward Smith
(1850–1912)

~

Capt. of RMS Titanic
Commander
Edward John Smith R.D. R.N.R.
Born January 27 1850 Died April 15 1912
Bequeathing to his countrymen
The memory & example of a great heart
A brave life and a heroic death.
Be British

Horatio, Lord Nelson
(1758–1805)

~

Sacred to the memory of
HORATIO LORD NELSON
Who, pious, brave, and fortunate,
Beloved by Men, and in peace with God,
Wanted nothing to complete the full measure
Of his glory,

But much to that of his reward;
Heaven and his country unite to discharge the debt;
Heaven by taking him to eternal happiness,
His country by devoting him to eternal remembrance.

Robert Louis Stevenson
(1850–94)
from his poem "Requiem" *1887*

~

Under the wide and starry sky
Dig the grave and let me lie.
Glad did I live and gladly die,
And I laid me down with a will.

This be the verse you grave for me:
Here he lies where he longed to be;
Home is the sailor, home from the sea
And the hunter from the hill.

President Garfield
(1831–81)
Assassinated

~

Life's race well run,
Life's work well done,
Life's victory won,
Now cometh rest.

Lucy Grove
(1747–87)

~

Grief, Love and Gratitude devote this stone
To her, whose virtues blest an husband's life.
When late in duty's sphere she mildly shone,
As friend, as sister, daughter, mother, wife.

In the bright morn of beauty, joy and wealth,
Insidious palsy near his victim drew;
Dash'd from her youthful hands the cup of health,
And round her limbs his numbing fetters threw.

Year after year her Christian firmness strove
To check the rising sigh, the tear repress,
Soothe with soft smiles the fears of anxious love,
And heaven's correcting hand in silence bless.

Thus tried her faith, and thus prepar'd her heart,
The awful call at length th' almighty gave:
She heard – resign'd to linger or depart,
Bow'd her meek head, and sunk into the grave.

Sir John Franklin
(1786–1847)
Arctic explorer

~

O ye Frost and Cold, O ye Ice and Snow
Bless ye the Lord Praise him and magnify him for
   ever.

Not here! The white North has thy bones; and
thou, heroic sailor-soul,
Art passing on thine happier voyage now
Toward no earthly pole.

Sir William Howard Russell
(1820–1907)

~

The first and greatest of war correspondents.

Robert Burns
(1759–96)

~

The poetic genius of my country found me
at the plough and threw her inspiring mantle over me.
She bade me sing the loves, the joys,
the rural scenes and rural pleasures of my native soil,
in my native tongue.
I tuned my wild, artless notes as she inspired.

King Alfred the Great
(849–99)

~

The mildest, justest, and most beneficent of Kings,
Who drove out the Danes, scour'd the Seas, promoted
   learning,
Established Juries, crush'd Corruption.
Guarded Liberty,
And was the Founder of the English Constitution.

George Gordon, Lord Byron
(1788–1824)

~

He died at Missolonghi, in Western Greece, on the
19th April, 1824,
Engaged in the glorious attempt to
restore that country to her ancient
freedom and renown.
His sister, the Honourable
Augusta Maria Leigh,
placed this tablet to his memory.

Ben Jonson
(1573–1637)

~

O rare
Ben Jonson

Captain Scott, Captain "Titus" Oates and others
(died 1912)

~

This Cross and Cairn are erected over the bodies of Capt. Scott, Dr E. Wilson, Lt H. Bowers, Royal Indian Marines. A slight token to perpetuate their gallant and successful attempt to reach the Pole. This they did on the 17th January 1912 after the Norwegian expedition had already done so. Inclement weather and lack of fuel was the cause of their death.

Also to commemorate their two gallant comrades, Capt L. Oates of the Inniskilling Dragoons, who walked to his death in a blizzard to save his comrades about 18 miles south of this position; also of Seaman

Edgar Evans, who died at the foot of the Beardmore Glacier.
The Lord gave and the Lord taketh away. Blessed be the name of the Lord.

Relief Expedition
(Signed by all members of the party.)

There is also a 1915 memorial to Captain Scott and team, sculpted by his widow and inscribed with these notes from his diary 22/23 March 1912:

. . . Had we lived, I should have had a tale to tell of the Hardihood, Endurance, and Courage of my companions which would have stirred the heart of every Englishman. These rough notes and our dead bodies must tell the tale.

David Garrick
(1716–79)

To paint fair nature, by divine command,
Her magic pencil in his glowing hand,
A Shakespeare rose; then, to expand his fame
Wide o'er this breathing world, a Garrick came:
Though sunk in death, the form the poet drew
The actor's genius bade them breathe anew;
Though like the bard himself, in night they lay,
Immortal Garrick call'd them back to day;
And till eternity with power sublime,
Shall mark the mortal hour of hoary time,
Shakespeare & Garrick, like twin stars shall shine,
And earth irradiate with beams divine.

George Washington
(1732–99)
Mount Vernon, Virginia

~

To the memory of the Man, first in war, first in
peace, and first in the hearts of his countrymen.

James Craggs
(1686–1721)
Secretary of State

~

Statesman, yet friend to Truth, of Soul sincere
In action faithful and in Honour clear
Who broke no Promise, serv'd no private end
Who gain'd no Title, and who lost no Friend
Ennobled by Himself, by all approv'd
Prais'd, wept and honour'd by the Muse he lov'd.

Cecil Day Lewis
(1904–72)

~

Shall I be gone long?
For ever and a day.
To whom there belong?
Ask the stone to say.
Ask my song.

David Hume
(1711–76)

~

Within this circular idea
Called vulgarly a tomb,
The ideas and impressions lie
That constituted Hume

John Okey
(1608–84)

~

The servant of God was born in London, 1608,
came into this town in 1629, married Mary, 1635,
with whom he lived comfortably 20 years
& begot 4 sons and 6 daughters.
Since then he lived sole till the day of his death.
In his time were many great changes & terrible
    alterations
– 18 years Civil War in England,
besides many dreadful sea fights –
the crown or command of England changed 8 times.
Episcopacy laid aside 14 years;
London burnt by Papists & more stately built again;
Germany wasted 300 miles;
200,000 Protestants murdered in Ireland, by the
    papists;
this town thrice stormed – once taken & plundered.
He went though many troubles and diverse
    conditions,
found rest, joy & happiness only in holiness
– the faith, fear and love of God in Jesus Christ.

D.H. Lawrence
(1885–1930)

~

Homo sum! the adventurer.

William Hogarth
(1697–1764)

~

Farewell, great Painter of mankind!
Who reached the noblest point of Art
Whose pictured Morals charm the Mind,
And through the Eye correct the Heart.

If Genius fire thee, Reader, stay:
If Nature touch thee, drop a Tear;
If neither move thee, turn away,
For HOGARTH'S honour'd dust lies here.

Vivien Leigh
(1913–67)

Actress

~

Now boast thee, death,
in thy possession lies
A lass unparallel'd

John Keats
(1795–1821)

~

This Grave
contains all that was Mortal
of a
YOUNG ENGLISH POET
Who
on his Death Bed,
in the Bitterness of his Heart
at the Malicious Power of his enemies,
desired
these Words to be engraved on his Tomb Stone.
"Here lies One
Whose name was writ in Water."

Sir Richard Burton
(1821–90)

~

Farewell, dear Friend, dead Hero!
The great life
is ended, the great perils, the great joys;
And he to whom adventures were as toys,
who seemed to bear a charm 'gainst spear or knife
or bullet, now lies silent from all strife
out yonder where the Austrian eagles poise
on Istrian hills, but England, at the noise
of that dread fall, weeps with the hero's wife.
Oh, last and noblest of the errant knights,
The English soldier and the Arab shiek!
Oh, singer of the East, who loved so well
The deathless wonder of the "Arabian Nights,"
Who touched Camoen's lute and still would seek
Ever new deeds until the end! Farewell!

Mrs Aphra Behn
(1640–89)

~

Here lies a Proof that Wit can never be
Defence enough against Mortality.

Edward George Lytton
(1803–73)

~

Laborious and distinguished in all fields of
   intellectual activity
indefatigable and ardent in the cultivation and love
   of letters
his genius as an author was displayed in the most
   varied forms
which have connected indissolubly
with every department of the literature of his time
the name of Edward Bulwer Lytton

Edmond Spencer
(1510–96)

~

Here lyes
(expecting the second Comminge of our Saviour
    Christ Jesus)
the body of Edmond Spencer, the Prince of Poets in
    his time;
whose divine spirit needs no other witness
than the works he left behind him.

David Livingstone
(1813–73)

~

Brought by faithful hands,
over land and sea,
here rests
David Livingstone,
Missionary,
Traveller,
Philanthropist.
Born March 19, 1813,

At Blantyre, Lanarkshire,
Died May 1, 1873,
At Chtittambo's village, Ulala.
For thirty years his life was spent
In an unwearied effort
To evangelise the native races
To explore the undiscovered secrets,
To abolish the desolating slave trade,
Of Central Africa,
Where with his last words he wrote,
"All I can add in my solitude, is,
May Heaven's rich blessing come down
on everyone, American, English or Turk
– who will help heal
this open sore of the world."

Cecil Rhodes
(1853–1902)

~

Your hinterland
is there.

Imogen Holst
(1907–84)

~

The
heavenly
spheres
make
music
for us.
All
things
join
in the dance.

Various
(died 1914–18)
Westminster Abbey

~

My Subject is War, and the pity of War,
The poetry is in the pity.
Richard Aldington, Laurence Binyon, Edmund

Blunden, Rupert Brooke, Wilfred Gibson, Robert
Graves, Julian Grenfell, Ivor Gurney, David Jones,
Robert Nichols, Wilfred Owen, Herbert Read, Isaac
Rosenberg, Siegfried Sassoon, Charles Sorley,
Edward Thomas   1914–1918

Harry St John Bridger Philby
(1885–1960)
Father of Kim Philby

∽

The Greatest Explorer of them all

Percy Bysshe Shelley
(1792–1822)

∽

COR CORDIUM
"Nothing of him that doth fade
But doth suffer a sea-change
Into something rich and strange."

∽ 143 ∽

John the Smith

(died 1371)

St Bartholomew, Brightwell Baldwin
Believed to be the earliest inscription in English

~

man com & se how schal alle ded li: wen yolk comes
    bad & bare

noth have ben ve away fare: All ys wermes y ve for
    care:-

bot y ve do for god ys luf ve haue nothyng yare:
    hundyr

yis graue lys John ye smyth god yif his soule hewn grit.

(Man, come and see how all dead men shall lie: when that
comes bad and bare, we have nothing when we away fare:
All that we care for is worms:– except for that which we do
for God's sake, we have nothing ready under this grave lies
John the Smith, God give his soul heavenly peace.)

William Shakespeare
(1564–1616)
Holy Trinity Church, Stratford-upon-Avon:

~

Good Friend for Jesus sake forbear,
To dig the dust enclosed here:
Blest be the man that spares these stones,
And curst be he that moves my bones.

Poets' Corner, Westminster Abbey:

~

The Cloud capt Tow'rs,
The Gorgeous Palaces,
The solemn Temples,
The Great Globe itself,
Yea, all which it Inherit,
Shall Dissolve,
And like the baseless Fabrick of a Vision
Leave not a wreck behind.
The Tempest (IV.i.152)

The Duke of Grafton
(17th century)

Here
Lies a peer
Beneath this place
Styl'd His Grace
The Duke of Grafton,
A blade as fine, as e'er had haft on.
Mark'd with a Garter and a Star,
Forg'd out and ground for war;
Of mettle true
As ever drew,
Or made a pass
At lad or lass.
This valiant son of Mars
ne'er hung an arse
With sword or tarse,
Nor turn'd his tail,
Tho' shots like hail
Flew about his ears
With spikes and spears
So thick, they'd hide the sun.
He boldly forc'd his way
Leading the van

More like the devil than a man:
For why, he valu'd not a fart a gun,
He ne'er would dread
Bullets of lead,
Nor cannon ball
Nothing at all;
But a bullet of cork
Soon did his work,
Unhappy pellet
With grief I tell it,
For with one blow thou has undone
Great Caesar's son:
A soldier foil'd,
A statesman spoil'd.
God rot him
That shot him
For a son of a whore,
I'll say no more,
But here lies Henry, Duke of Grafton.

Alexander Pope
(1688–1744)

~

For one who would not be buried in Westminster Abbey

Heroes and Kings! your distance keep;
In peace let one poor Poet sleep,
Who never flatter'd Folks like you:
Let Horace blush, and Virgil too.

Elizabeth Pepys
(1640–69)

~

Wife of Samuel Pepys (who serves the Royal Navy).
She was educated first in a convent, and then in a
     seminary of France.
She was distinguished by the excellence of both at
     once,
Gifted with beauty, accomplishments, tongues,
She bore no offspring, for she could not have borne
     her life.

At length when she had bidden this world a gentle
    farewell,
(After a journey completed through, we may say, the
    lovelier sights of Europe) –
A returning pilgrim, she took her departure to
    wander through a grander world.

Karl Marx
(1818–83)

~

Workers of all Lands
Unite

The philosophers have only
interpreted the world in
various ways. The point
however is to change it.

Samuel Butler
(1612–80)

~

Sacred to the memory of

SAMUEL BUTLER,

Who was born at Strensham, in Worcestershire, 1612 and died in London 1680; a man of uncommon wit and probity: as admirable for the product of his genius, as unhappy in the rewards of them. His satire, exposing the hypocrisy and wickedness of the rebels, is such an inimitable piece, that as he was the first, he may be said to be the last writer in this peculiar manner. That he, who, when living, wanted almost everything, might not, after death, any longer want so much as a tomb, JOHN BARBER, citizen of London, erected this monument 1721.

The Duke of Buckingham
(17th century)

~

Here lies the best and worst of fate,
Two kings' delight, the people's hate,
The courtier's star, the kingdom's eye,
A man to draw an angel by,
Fear's despiser, Villiers' glory,
The great man's volume, all time's story.

James Baskerville
(1706–75)

~

Stranger
Beneath this cone in unconsecrated ground
a friend to the liberties of mankind directed his body
    to be inurn'd
May the example contribute to emancipate thy mind
From the idle fears of Superstition
And the wicked arts of Priesthood

Thomas Gray
(1716–71)

~

This Monument, in honour of
Thomas Gray
Was erected AD 1799
Among the scenery
Celebrated by that great Lyric and Elegiac Poet.
He died in 1771
And lies unnoticed in the adjoining Churchyard;
Under the tombstone
On which he piously and pathetically
Recorded the interment
Of his Aunt and lamented Mother

Patrick Henry
(1736–99)
American statesman

~

His fame is his best epitaph.

Kenneth Grahame
(1859–1932)

~

To
the beautiful memory
of Kenneth Grahame
Husband of Elspeth
and
Father of Alastair
who passed the river
on the 6th of July 1932
leaving
Childhood and literature
through him the more blest
for all time.

Mary Herbert, Countess of Pembroke
(1561–1621)

~

Underneath this sable Herse
Lies the Subject of all Verse:
Sydney's Sister, Pembroke's Mother –
Death! ere thou Kill'st such another
Fair, and good, and learnd as SHEE,
Time will throw his Dart at thee.

Charles Watson Wentworth
(1730–82)

~

Charles Watson Wentworth
Marquis of Rockingham, Earl of Malton,
Viscount Higham of Higham Ferrers,
Baron of Buckingham, Malton, Wath and
Harowden and Baronet in Great Britain,
Earl and Baron of Malton in the
Kingdom of Ireland, Lord Lieutenant and
Custos Rotulorum of the West Riding
Of Yorkshire, City of York and County
of the same, Custos Rotulorum of the

North Riding, and Vice Admiral of the
Maritime parts therof, High Steward
of Kingston upon Hull, Knight of the
Garter and first Commissioner of the
Board of Treasury.

Thomas Redhead
(1757–1839)
St Augustine, Burrough Green

~

Who in his pursuits in life was successful
In his enjoyment of Fortune, moderate:
In his intercourse with his friends, truthful, just and
    sincere.
Beloved by his servants and dependents.
In his last protracted illness he
suffered pain with patient submission
to the will of God: and died in the
Hope of Salvation: through the merits
Of his Great Redeemer.

Andrew Marvell
(1621–78)

~

Near unto this place lyeth the body of Andrew
    Marvell Esquire,
a man so endowed by nature,
so improved by education, study & travel,
so consummated by practice & experience;
that joining the most peculiar graces of wit &
    learning
with a singular penetration & strength of judgment
& exercising all these in the whole course of his life,
with an unalterable steadiness in the ways of virtue,
he became the ornament and example of his age;
beloved by good men, feared by bad, admir'd by all,
though imitated alas by few
& scarce fully paralleled by any,
but a tombstone can neither contain his character,
nor is marble necessary to transmit it to posterity,
it will always be legible in his inimitable writings,
he served the town of Kingston upon Hull above 20
    years
successively in Parliament & that,
with such wisdom, dexterity, integrity
and courage as becomes a true patriot.

Richard Peyton
(1534–74)
St Andrew, Isleham

~

Here under lyeth a worthy Squire that Richard Peyton
hight

An Honest Gentleman & third Sonne to Robert
Peyton Knight.

In Grays Inn Student of the Law, where he a Reader
was,

He feared God and loved his Word, in Truth his Life
did pass.

In practising of Justice, Love was all his whole delight:

He never wronged anyone, to whom he might do Right.

Whom he esteemed an honest Friend, whom he might
stand in Stead

He never left to do him good, with Word, with Purse
and Deed.

For ten years Space he married was unto a faithful
Wife

By Parent named Mary Hyde they lived devoid of
Strife:

The Earth him bare twice Twenty years and virtuously
he lived;

A godly Life he did embrace and virtuously he died.

Sir Kenelm Digby
(1603–65)

~

Under this tomb the Matchless Digby lies,
Digby the Great, the Valiant and the Wise
This Age's Wonder, for his Noble Parts,
Skill'd in six Tongues, and learn'd in all the Arts;
Born on the day he Died, th' Eleven of June
And that day bravely fought at SCANDEROON.
It's Rare, that one and the same day should be
His day of Birth, of Death, of Victory!

Richard Scarlet
(1496–1594)
Peterborough Cathedral

~

You see old Scarlet's picture stand on high
But at your feet there doth his body lye.
His gravestone doth his age and death-time show,
His office by these tokens you may know;
Second to none for strength, and sturdy limb,

A scarbabe mighty voice with visage grim;
he had interred two queens within this place;
And this town's householders in his life's space
Twice over; but at length his own turn came
What he for others did, for him the same
Was done: no doubt his soul doth live for aye
in Heaven, though here his body lies in clay.

Anne Kemp, Lady Cutt
(1583–1631)
St Andrew, Swavesey

∼

Wise-Good; Faire-Chaste; these matched in One
Dissolved by Heaven, by Heaven alone
Shall, at this passing World's new birth
Be matched again with that RARE EARTH
Which here by common earth possessed
Attends the call of COME YE BLESSED

Mary Relict
(died 1692)
Coleshill, Warwickshire

~

Whom it were unpardonable to lay down in silence
and of whom it is difficult to speak with justice.
For her just character will look like flattery
and the least abatement of this injury to her memory.
In every condition of life she was a pattern to her sex,
appeared mistress of those peculiar qualities
that were requisite to conduct her through it with
    honour,
and never failed to exert them in their proper seasons
with the utmost advantage.
She was modest without affectation,
easy without levity and reserved without pride;
knew how to stoop without sinking
and to gain people's affections without lessening their
    regards.
She was careful without anxiety, frugal without
    parsimony;
not at all fond of the superfluous trappings of
    greatness,
yet abridged herself in nothing that her quality
    required.

She was a faithful member of the Church of England,
her piety was exemplary, her charity universal.
She found herself a widow at the beginning of her life
when the temptations of Beauty, honour, youth,
and pleasure were in their full strength;
yet she made them all give way to the interest of her
    family
and betook herself entirely of the matron's part . . .
In a word she was truly wise, truly honourable and
    truly good.
More can scarce be said,
and yet he that says this knew her well
and is well assured he has said nothing
which either veracity or modesty
should oblige him to suppress.

Ann Cotton
(1702–21)
St Mary, Conington

Here lyeth the Body of Mrs Ann Cotton
Whose cheerful Temper and agreeable Virtue
Made the Beauty of her Person her least
    Commendation:
Though these were so sweetly united
That they mutually advanced each other:
For from her Virtues
Her person received a new Loveliness
As they from that, an additional Lustre.
She lived so well
That there remained nothing to make her perfect but
    to die
Her sickness was short
But Death did not surprize her
Who could cheerfully resign her Spirit
At a Time
When it is greater Glory to part with this World
    willingly
than to possess it innocently.
The Reward of her Virtues remains to herself
The Example of them to us.

John Donne
(1572–1631)

Reader, I am to let thee know,
Donne's body only lies below;
For could the grave his soul comprise,
Earth would be richer than the skies.

King Arthur
(*c.* 1450)

~

"Here lies Arthur, the once and future king"

Jerome K. Jerome
(1859–1927)

~

In loving remembrance
of
Jerome Klapka Jerome.
Died June 14th 1927.
Aged 68 years.
"For we are labourers together with God."

Jack and Joan
(17th century)

~

Interr'd beneath this marble stone
Lie Saunt'ring JACK and Idle JOAN,
While rolling threescore years and one
did round this globe their courses run;
If human things went ill or well;
If changing empires rose or fell;
The morning past, the evening came,
And found this couple still the same.
They walk'd and eat, good folks: What then?
Why then they walk'd and eat again:
They soundly slept the night away:
They did just nothing all the day:
And having buried children four,
Would not take pains to try for more.
Nor sister either had, nor brother:
They seemed just tallied for each other.
Their moral and economy
Most perfectly they made agree:
Each virtue kept its proper bound,
Nor trespass'd on the other's ground.
Nor fame, nor censure they regarded:
They neither punish'd nor rewarded.

He car'd not what the footmen did:
Her maids she neither prais'd nor chid:
So ev'ry servant took his course;
And bad at first they all grew worse.
Slothful disorder fill'd his stable
And sluttish plenty deck'd her table.
Their beer was strong; their wine was port;
Their meal was large; their grace was short.
they gave the poor the remnant-meat,
Just when it grew not fit to eat.

They paid the church and parish rate:
And took but read not the receipt:
For which they claim'd their Sunday's due,
Of slumbering in an upper pew.

No man's defects sought they to know
So never made themselves a foe.
No man's good deeds did they commend;
So never rais'd themselves a friend.

Nor cherish'd they relations poor:
That might decrease their present store:
Nor barn nor house did they repair:
That might oblige their future heir.

They neither added nor confounded:
They neither wanted, nor abounded.
Each Christmas they accounts did clear;
And wound their bottom round the year.
Nor tear, nor smile did they employ
At news of public grief or joy

When bells were rung and bonfires made
If ask'd they ne'er denied their aid:
Their jug was to the ringers carried.
Whoever either died or married.
Their billet at the fire was found,
Whoever was depos'd or crown'd.

Nor good nor bad nor fools nor wise
They would not learn nor could advise:
Without love, hatred, joy or fear,
They led – a kind of – as it were:
Nor wish'd, nor car'd, nor laugh'd, nor cried:
And so they liv'd and so they died.

George Eliot
(pseudonym of Mary Ann Evans)
(1819–80)

~

"Of those immortal dead who live again
In minds made better by their presence"

Here lies the body
of "George Eliot"
Mary Ann Cross

Phoebe Hessel
(1713–1821)

~

Phoebe Hessel
Who was born in Stepney in the year 1713
She served for many years
as a private soldier in the 5th Regt of foot
in different parts of Europe
and in the year 1745 fought under the command
of the Duke of Cumberland
at the battle of Fontenoy
where she received a Bayonet wound in her Arm.

Her long life which commenced in the time of
Queen Anne
extended to the reign of
George IV
by whose munificence she received comfort
and support in her later Years
she died at Brighton, where she had long resided,
December 12th. 1821 Aged 108 years

Viscountess Downe
(died 1812)

~

A real unpretending and almost unconscious good
    sense and
a firm desire to act right on all occasions to the best
of her judgment were her most distinguished
Characteristics, hereditary personal grace of both
    form
and face which even in age had not disappeared
    completes
her picture. For her character and other particulars
    see
the Gentleman's Magazine for May 1812.

Samuel Foote
(1720–77)

~

Here lies one foote, whose death may thousands save,
For death has now one foot within the grave.

Arthur Conan Doyle
(1859–1930)

~

Steel True
Blade Straight
Arthur Conan Doyle
Knight
Patriot, Physician & Man of Letters

Mary, Lady Curzon
(1870–1906)

Perfect in Love and Loveliness
Beauty was the least of her rare gifts
God had endowed with like graces
Her mind and soul had
From illness almost unto death
Restored only to die
She was mourned in three continents
and by her dearest
will be
for ever unforgotten.

George Rongleigh
(1800-57)

～

Here lies in a horizontal position
The outside case of George Rongleigh, watchmaker,
Whose abilities in that line were an honor
to his profession.
Integrity was the mainspring
and Prudence the Regulator
of all the actions of his life;
Humane, Generous and Liberal,
His Hand never stopped
Till he had relieved distress:
So nicely were all his Actions regulated
That he never went wrong,
Except when set going
By People
who did not know his key:
Even then he was easily set right again.
He had the art of disposing his time so well
That his hours glided away
In one continual round
of pleasure and delight,
Till an unlucky minute put a period to
his existence.

He departed this life November 14th 1802,
Aged 57
Wound up
In hopes of being taken in hand
by his maker,
And of being thoroughly cleaned and repaired,
and set going
In the World to come.

Christopher Jeaffreson
(1699–1748)
St Mary, Dullingham

~

He wrongs the Dead who thinks this Marble Frame
Was set to be the Guardian of his name
Whereas 'twas for his Ashes only meant
His Name was set to guard the Monument.

M.H.
(17th century)

~

In this cold monument lies one,
That I knew who has lain upon,
The happier He; her sight would charm,
And touch have kept King David warm.
Lovely, as is the dawning East,
Was this marble's frozen guest;
As soft, and snowy, as that down
Adorns Blow-ball's frizzled crown;
And straight and slender as the crest,
or antlet of the one-beamed beast;
Pleasant as th'odorous month of May:
As glorious, as the light of Day.

Whom I admire'd, as soon as knew,
And nowhere memory pursue
With such a superstitious lust,
That I could fumble with her dust.

She all perfections had and more,
Tempting, as if design'd a whore,
For so she was; and since there are
Such, I would wish them all as fair.

Pretty she was, and young and wise,
And in her calling so precise,
That industry had made her prove
The suckingschool-mistress of love:
And Death, ambitious to become
Her pupil, left his ghastly home,
And seeing how we us'd her here,
The raw-boned rascal ravisht her.

Who pretty Soul, resign'd her breath,
To seek new lechery in Death.

Jonathan Swift
(1667–1745)

~

Here lies the body of Jonathan Swift, Professor of
    Holy Theology,
Dean of this cathedral church,
where savage indignation can tear his heart no longer.
Go, traveller,
and if you can imitate one who with his utmost
    strength protected liberty.

Sir John Ellys
(1630–1716)
St Mary, Swaffham Prior

~

Here by his order lies Sir John Ellys Knight
Dr of Physic and Master of Gonville and Caius
    College in Cambridge
where Queen Anne of Blessed Memory knighted him
being Vice-Chancellor AD 1705.
He then defended the Privileges for that University
with Courage, Prudence and Success.
In his post of Master of Caius College for about 14
    years,
the Promoter of True Religion, good Morals, regular
    Discipline and Useful Learning
were the ends of the College
and University Statues with the Laws of the Land the
    Rules of his Government.
While Fellow he was for about 40 years a Tutor
eminent for Piety, Virtue, Learning, Diligence and
    Integrity.
And admirable Method of Instruction, Exemplary
    conversation,
constant keeping Chapel, Church and Lectures
and Care his Pupils should do the like.

By his interest he Procured Several Considerable
    Benefactors to the College
and about 1695 gave them fifty Pounds towards
    their Buying
the Advowson of Broadmay in Dorsetshire.
In all the stages of his Life he was a true friend.
Temperate in all things, humble, meek, sincere and
    obliging,
Charitable and Generous.

The memory of the Righteous shall be blessed.

Rupert Brooke
(1887–1915)

~

If I should die, think only this of me:
That there's some corner of a foreign field
That is for ever England, there shall be
In that rich earth a richer dust concealed;
A dust whom England bore, shaped, made aware,
Gave, once, her flowers to love, her ways to roam,
A body of England's, breathing English air,
Washed by the rivers, blest by suns of home,
And think, this heart, all evil shed away,
A pulse in the eternal mind, no less
Gives somewhere back the thoughts by England
    given,
Her sights and sounds; Dreams happy as her day;
And laughter, learnt of friends; and Gentleness,
In hearts at peace, under an English heaven.

Jacob Epstein
(1880–1959)

~

From life's grim nightmare he is now released
Who saw in every face the lurking beast.
"A loss to Art," say friends both proud and loyal,
"A loss," say others, "to the Cafe Royal."

William Inglott
(died 1621)

~

Here William Inglott organist doth rest
Whose art in musique this cathedral blest.
For descant most, for voluntary all
He past: organ, songe and virginall.
He left this life at age of thirtie seven
And now amongst angels all sings saints in heaven
His fame flies far, his name shall never die
See art and age here crown his memory.

Henry Clemetshaw
(1753–1821)

~

In memory of
Henry Clemetshaw
upwards of fifty years organist
of this church, who died
May 7, 1821, aged 68 years.
Now, like an organ, robb'd of pipes and breath,
Its keys and stops are useless made by death,
Tho' mute and motionless in ruins laid,
Yet when re-built by more than mortal aid,
This instrument, new voiced and tuned shall raise
To God, its builder, hymns of endless praise.

Joseph Addison
(1672–1719)
Westminster Abbey

~

Ne'er to these chambers, where the mighty rest,
Since their foundation, came a nobler guest;
Nor e'er was to the bowers of bliss conveyed

A fairer spirit, or more welcome shade!
Oh, gone for ever! take this long adieu,
And sleep in peace next thy lord Montague.

Henry Purcell
(1658–95)
Westminster Abbey

Here lyes
Henry Purcell Esqr.
who left this life
And is gone to that blessed place
Where only his Harmony
can be exceeded

Jane Austen
(1775–1817)

~

In Memory of Jane Austen
youngest daughter of the late
Revd George,
formerly Rector of Steventon in this County,
she departed this Life on the 18th of July, 1817,
aged 41, after a long illness supported with
the patience and the hopes of a Christian.

The benevolence of her heart,
the sweetness of her temper,
and the extraordinary endowments of her mind
obtained the regard of all who knew her, and
the warmest love of her intimate connections.

Their grief is in proportion to their affection,
they know their loss to be irreparable,
but in their deepest affliction they are consoled
by a firm though humble hope that her charity,
devotion, faith and purity, rendered
her soul acceptable in the sight of her
REDEEMER.

Alfred Jopling Cooper
(1847–1923)

∿

He discovered the solectric theory which
enables us to understand the forces which
are acting to cause natural phenomena
earthquakes, violent storms, tornadoes, etc.

The negative circle of intense solectric force
has a radius on earth's surface of 57 1/2 degrees:
The positive circle has a radius of 88 degrees.

He predicted the Valparaiso earthquake
of Aug:16:1906, and he also predicted in the
Valparaiso "Mercurio" of Oct:10: as confirmed
in Page 7 of "The Times" of Dec:7:1918, the
day and hour of the Chilean earthquake
of Dec:4:1918, hence 8 weeks before its
occurrence.

Charles Villiers Stanford
(1852–1924)

~

SIR

CHARLES

VILLIERS

STANFORD

Born 30th Sept 1852

Died 29th March 1924

A Great Musician

Mary Maltby
(1771–1825)
St Mary, Buckden

~

If tender feeling for another's woe
If resignation in her own bestow
A claim on pity and invite a tear
Weep, Stranger, weep upon her honoured bier!
If each domestic charm, each virtue mild
That graced the Parent, Sister, Wife and Child
Wisdom in fair Example's form supply
Then learn like her to live and hope like her to die.

Agneta Yorke
(1739–1820)
St Andrew, Wimpole

In youth she was most lovely,
In womanhood most dignified
In old age most venerable
It was truly said of her in her prime
That it was difficult which to admire most
The beauty of her virtue or the virtue of her beauty.
In her breast were united the tenderness of an
 Englishwoman
And the spirit of a Roman matron.
The faculties and endowments of her mind were of
 the highest order
Her opinions, her principles, all the sentiments of her
 heart
Were sincere, upright and noble.
Her whole life was that of a real Christian
Pious without austerity and charitable without
 ostentation
May I die the death of the righteous
And may my latter end be like hers.

James Fortrey
(1656–1719)
St Mary, Mepal

~

Near this place lie the remains of James Fortrey
    Esquire
descended from an ancient stock in Brabant:
which took an asylum in England from the
    persecution
of the Spaniards in the reign of Queen Elizabeth.
He was 3rd son of Samuel Fortrey Esq
who upon undertaking the draining of the Bedford
    Level
erected a commodious habitation in Byal Fen
which coming into his son's possession
was by him enlarged with several commodious
    apartments
with gardens and other improvements so as to make it
(a Place in such a Situation)
the admiration of the time.

He was bred in Courts and in Camp,
was Page of Honour to Mary of Modena,
then Dutchess of York,
afterwards Groom of the Bedchamber to her husband

King James the 2nd,
Major in the Horse Guards and at the same time
    commanded
a troop in Laniers Regiment of the Horse.

He would have followed his unhappy royal Master's
    fortune in exile
but was forbidden by his command on the account of
    his ill health.
Fidelity and gratitude forbad him to engage in the
    service of his successor.

Having lived a favourite of Princes he rather chose
    Obscurity
and after residing some time as Fellow Commoner
at Queen's College in Cambridge
passed the remainder of his days
in retirement between Portugal and Byal Fen.

Joseph Conrad
(1857–1924)

~

Sleep after toile, port after stormie seas,
Ease after warre, death after life, does greatly please.

Lancelot Brown
(1716–83)
St Peter and St Paul, Fenstanton

~

Ye sons of Elegance who truly taste
The Simpler Charms that genuine Art supplies
Come from the Sylvan Scenes His Genius grac'd
And offer here your tributary Sighs.
But know that more than Genius slumbers here
Virtues were his which Art's best powers transcend
Come, ye Superior train who these revere
And weep the Christian, Husband, Father, Friend.

Philip Roe
(1763–1815)

~

Erected
In remembrance of
Philip Roe
who died 12th September 1815
Aged 52 years
The vocal powers here let us mark
Of Philip our late Parish Clerk
In Church none ever heard a layman
With a clearer Voice say "Amen!"
Who now with Hallelujahs Sound
Like Him can make the Roofs rebound?
The Choir lament his choral Tones
The Town – so soon Here lie his Bones.
"Sleep undisturb'd within thy peaceful shrine
Till Angels wake thee with such notes as thine."

Thomas Woodward
(1702–69)

~

Here lies the Body
Of Thomas Woodward, Surgeon
of Piccadilly
who departed this life Sept 23, 1769
He was Eminent for the Knowledge of
Surgery, having made that Science
His Study for upwards of Forty Years.
In the cure of Ruptures he surpassed all
the Faculty in the Age he Lived.
And all Past Ages, as many thousands
of all Ranks who have been Cured
by his Medicines and Bandages can Ivince.
The poor afflicted with that Disorder
He Cured gratis.

Elizabeth, Countess of Aboyne
(1800–39)
Holy Trinity, Orton Longueville

~

Tho' gifted with mental Powers and Personal
  Attractions
to grace the most brilliant circles of public Society,
in home and its sweet Association
she sought and found her tranquil joys.
The buoyancy of her Spirits at seeming variance
with such Habits of deep Reflection,
the playfulness of her wit in rare harmony
with such strength of Judgment
her delicacy of feeling, her amiableness of
  Disposition
her Excellence in every relation of Life
her surpassing Worth in the most Tender
these are recorded on fleshly tablets and deepest
  graven His sorrowing Heart
who fondly dedicates this Monument to her dear
  Memory.

Samuel Johnson
(1709–84)

~

Under this Stone
rest the Remains of Samuel Johnson,
afterwards ennobled with the grander title of
    Lord Flame.
Who, after having been in his Life distinct from
    other men,
By the eccentricities of his Genius,
chose to retain the same Character after his death.
And was on his own desire buried here May 5th.

Stay thou whom chance or ease persuades to seek the
    quiet of these sylvan shades.
here undisturbed hid from vulgar eyes, a wit,
    musician, poet, player lies.
A dancing master too in grace he shone, and all the
    arts of opera were his own.
In comedy well skilled, he drew Lord Flame; acted
    the part and gained
himself the name.

Averse to strife how oft he'd gravely say, these
    peaceful groves should shade his breathless day.

That when he rose again laid here alone, no friend
     and he should quarrel for a bone.
Thinking that were some old lame gossip nigh, she
     possibly might take his leg or thigh.

Benjamin Franklin
(1706–90)

~

The body of
B. Franklin,
Printer,
Like the cover of an old book
its contents torn out,
and stripped of its lettering and gilding,
lies here, food for worms.
But the work shall not be wholly lost,
for it will, as he believed, appear once more,
in a new and more perfect edition,
corrected and amended
by the Author.

Henry Barratt
(1798–1841)
All Saints, Hartford

~

Unknown to fame nor wishing to be known
Yet sleeps beneath this monumental stone
No common man: and ne'er was record set
O'er one more worth an honest heart's regret.
Above each sordid aim, each selfish fear
Warm to a few, to all the world sincere
Paying no homage to the seeming great
But prizing genuine worth in every state
With taste unerring skilful to descry
The sterling gold and cast the tinsel by,
No merit owning save what bore the test
Of truth which sparkled in his ready jest.
If life's meridian years too early lost
The friends who, knowing best deplore him most
Have rais'd this tomb 'mid' scenes he loved to grace
To mark their old companion's resting place.

Edward Marshall
(1562–1625)
St Andrew, Wimpole

A shining star that glittered far when fixed in this our
skie
A radiant light shew'd to our sight of Knowledge
from on hie
And by his motion gave direction how we should
move on earth
His influence store of alms ye poore in need receiv'd
& dearth
By many prayers and showering tears this place his
influence had
Of comfort much and blessings such as joyed and
made yet glad
This star so bright hath lost his light being fallen in
the ground
His earth we have within this grave his Soul in
Heaven is crowned.

William Pickering (1795–1845) and
Richard Edger (1821–45)
Engine driver and his mate

~

The Spiritual Railway
The Line to Heaven by Christ was made
With heavenly truth the Rails are laid.
From earth to heaven the line extends,
To life Eternal where it ends.
Repentance is the Station then
Where Passengers are taken in.
No fee is there for them to pay,
For Jesus is himself the way.
God's Word is the first Engineer
He points the way to Heaven so dear,
Through tunnels dark and dreary here
It does the way to Glory steer.
God's Love the fire, his Truth the Steam,
Which drives the Engine and the Train.
All you who would to glory ride,
Must come to Christ, in him abide.
In First, and Second and Third Class,
Repentance, Faith and Holiness.
You must the way to Glory gain
Or you with Christ will not remain.

Come then poor Sinners, now's the time
At any station on the Line.
If you'll repent and turn from sin
The Train will stop and take you in.

John Higgs
(dates unknown)

~

Here lies John Higgs
A famous man for killing pigs.
For killing pigs was his delight
Both morning afternoon and night.
Both heat and cold he did endure
Which no Physician could cure.
His knife is laid his work is done
I hope to heaven his soul is gone.

William Wheatley

(1685–1723)

St Mary and St Andrew, Whittlesford

~

Near this place lies the Body of Mr Will Wheatley of
Cambridge, Grocer.

He married Lucy, by whom he had Issue

Robert, Elizabeth, Richard, William, Lucy,
Biddulph, William and William

who all died in their infancy and lie buried near their
Father.

He was in his life time an Encourager of the Charity
Schools in Cambridge

and seeing the good effects of that most excellent
Charity,

he generously left his 2 Farms of Hempstead in Essex

for the founding of a Charity School in Whittlesford

the Place of his Birth and Seat of his Family,

out of a pious Design to have the children of the
Poor,

educated in the fear of God

and instructed in the Principles of the Christian
Religion,

that they might become faithful Servants of God

and sincere Members of his Holy Church.

This monument was erected at the Charge of his
    Widow
the better to preserve the Memory of her deceased
    Husband
of this excellent Charity
and to set thee an
Example, Reader, to go and do likewise.

Herbert Henry Asquith
(1852–1928)

~

Unmoved,
Unshaken, unseduced, unterrified,
His Loyalty he kept, his Love, his Zeal;
Nor number, nor example with him wrought
To swerve from truth, or change his constant mind.

Sir Thomas Beecham
(1879–1961)

~

Nothing can cover
his high fame but
Heaven. No pyramids
set off his memories
but the eternal
substance of his
greatness.

Matthew Boulton
(1728–1809)

~

By the skilful exertion of a mind turned to
    philosophy and mechanics,
the application of a taste correct and refined,
and an ardent spirit of enterprise,
he embellished and extended
the arts and manufacture of his country,
leaving his establishment of Soho

a noble monument of his genius, industry and
success.
The character his talents had raised,
his virtues adorned and exalted.
Active to discover merit,
and prompt to relieve distress,
His encouragement was liberal,
his benevolence unwearied.
Honoured and admired at home and abroad
he closed a life eminently useful,
the 17th of August 1809 aged 81
Esteemed, loved and lamented.

Hilaire Belloc
(1870–1953)

~

When I am dead, I hope it may be said:
"His sins were scarlet, but his books were read."

Viscount Knutsford
(1855–1931)
St Peter and St Paul, Bassingbourn

~

Chairman for 35 years of the London Hospital.
His lifelong work was devoted to the relief
of suffering and the advance of medical science.
His joy was to help all in distress and to
bring happiness into the lives of others.
"Inasmuch as ye have done it unto one of the least
of these my brethren ye have done it unto me."

James Watt
(1736–1819)

~

James Watt
Not to perpetuate a name
Which must endure while the peaceful arts flourish,
But to show
That mankind have learned to honour those
Who best deserve their gratitude,

The King
His Ministers and many of the Nobles
and Commons of the Realm,
Raised this monument to
James Watt
Who, directing the force of original genius,
early exercised in Philosophic research
To the improvement of
The Steam Engine
Enlarged the resources of his country,
Increased the power of man
And rose to an eminent place
Among the most illustrious followers of science
And the real Benefactors of the world.

Commander Charles Cotton R.N.
(1803–28)
St Mary Magdalene, Madingley

~

who died on board of H.M.S. Zebra in the
    Mediterranean
and was interred near the Pratique Church at Malta,
where a Monument erected by his officers and men
attested with their own grief their deep sense of his
    loss to the service.
He was the youngest son of Sir Charles Cotton Bart
and having embraced his father's profession
he displayed that zeal and talent
which secured for him the high approbation of his
Commander-in-Chief and the confidence of those
    that served with him.
His death was occasioned by a fever
resulting from the fatigues of an arduous service
in which he was conspicuous
in rescuing the crew of H.M.S. Cambrian off
    Carabusa
in the Island of Candia.

Chapter 4

~·❦·~

FUNNY (AND PECULIAR)

Some of these are short, some are almost certainly apocryphal and some are just plain bizarre.

Name and date unknown

～

Here lies a lewd Fellow, who, while he drew Breath,
In the Midst of his Life was in Quest of his Death;
Which he quickly obtain'd for it cost him his Life,
For being in Bed with another Man's Wife.

Robert Philip
(died 1793)
St Andrew, Isleham

～

Here lie I at the Chancel door
Here lie I because I'm poor
The further in the more you'll pay
Here lie I as warm as they.

Mary Henson
(1694–1719)
St Andrew, Caxton

～

Here lieth the body of Mary Henson.
She was married to John Henson Junior
of Sawtrey in the County of Huntingdon 25th April
    1718,
her husband died in June following
and left her with child
and she was brought to bed January 21st after
and died February 3rd after that,
aged about 25 years,
so in the compass of less than ten months
she was a maid, a wife, a widow, a mother and died.

Thus in these tender climes where oft we see
Ripe fruit and Blossoms on the Same Fair Tree
Some cruel Blast, the various Scene annoys
And with the ready Cross, our Hope destroys.

Merry Pitman
(1793–1857)
*Wife of Isaac Pitman,
inventor of Pitman shorthand system*

~

In memori ov
MERI PITMAN
Fonetik Printer, ov this Siti.
Died 19 August 1857, edjed 64.
"Preper tu mit thei God."
– Emos 4–12

Thomas Jetherell
(died June 1774)
All Saints, Huntingdon

~

He was an example of piety during his life,
and of honesty at his death
And tho' a Bankruptcy brought his
character for a while under a cloud
His religion inspired him

with Sentiment at last
to dissipate it
by bequeathing all his after acquisitions
which were considerable
to his Creditors
to whom his conscience only could determine them
    due
That if he scandalised the world
by some miscarriages
he hath instructed it by repairing
them to the utmost of his power
Who chose rather to leave
His relations in want
than transmit to them
a patrimony of malediction
and give them an example of equity
rather than the fruit of injustice

Go thou and do likewise

William Simmonds
(1673–1753)
St Mary, Wood Ditton

~

Here lies my corpse who was the man
That lov'd a sop in dripping pan
But now believe me I am dead
Now here the pan stands at my head
Still for sop to the last I cry'd
But could not eat and so I died
My neighbours they perhaps may laugh
When they do read my epitaph.

William Young
(1841–61)

~

William Young was killed by the bells of this church.

Nicholas Toke
(18th century)
Great Chart, Kent

❧

He married five wives
Whom he survived.
At the age of 93 he walked to London
to seek a sixth but died before he found her.

Name and dates unknown

❧

Since thy third curing of the French infection,
Priapus hath in thee found no erection,
yet eat'st thou ringoes and potato roots
And caviar, but it little boots.
Besides the bed's head a bottle's lately found
Of liquor that a quart cost twenty pound:
For shame, if not more grace, yet shew more wit
Surcease now sin leaves thee to follow it.
Some smile, I sigh, to see thy madness such
That that which stands not, stands thee in so much.

John Gill
(dates unknown)

~

Beneath this smooth stone by the bone of his bone
Sleeps Master John Gill;
By lies when alive this attorney did thrive,
And now that he's dead he lies still.

John Cruker
(dates unknown)
Bellows maker of Oxford

~

Here lieth John Cruker, a maker of bellows,
His craft's master, and king of good fellows;
yet when he came to the hour of his death,
He that made bellows, could not make breath.

John Partridge
(18th century)
Astrologer and almanac maker

Here, five feet deep, lies on his back
A cobbler, star-monger, and quack;
Who, to the stars in pure good will,
Does to his best look upward still.
Weep, all you customers, that use
His pills, his almanacs, or shoes:
And you, that did your fortunes seek,
Step to his grave but once a week:
This earth, which bears his body's print,
You'll find has so much virtue in't,
That I durst pawn my ears, 'twill tell
Whate'er concerns you full as well,
In physic, stolen goods, or love,
As he himself could, when above.

Mr Pricke
(dates unknown)

~

Upon the fifth day of November
Christ's College lost a privy member;
Cupid and death did both their arrows nick,
Cupid shot short, but death did hit the prick;
Women lament and maidens make great moans,
Because the prick is laid beneath the stones.

Name unknown
(17th century)

~

Here lies a great sleeper as everybody knows
Whose soul would not care if his body ne'er rose,
The business of life he hated and chose
To die for his ease for his better repose;
And 'tis believed, when the last trump doth wake him
Had the Devil a bed, he would pray him to take him.

Jacob Tonson
(17th century)
Publisher

∼

With leering looks, bullfac'd and freckled fair,
With two left legs and Judas-colour'd hair,
With frowzy pores, that taint the ambient air.

Elizabeth Alleyn
(died 1652)
Great Witchingham, Norfolk

∼

Death here advantage hath of life I spy
One husband with 2 wifes at once may lie.

Emily White
(20th century)
Huddersfield

∼

Here lies the body of Emily White,
She signalled left, and then turned right.

John Dale
(1651–1737)

~

Know posterity that the rambling remains
of the above said John Dale
were in the 86th year of his pilgrimage,
laid upon his two wives.

This thing in life might raise some jealousy,
Here all three lie together lovingly,
But from embraces here no pleasure flows,
Alike are here all human joys and woes;
Here Sarah's chiding John no longer hears,
And old John's rambling Sarah no more fears;
A period's come to all their toilsome lives,
The good man's quiet; still are both his wives.

W.C. Fields
(1880–1946)

Here lies W.C. Fields.
On the whole I would rather be living in
Philadelphia.

Groucho Marx
(1895–1977)

Here lies Groucho Marx
and Lies and Lies and Lies
P.S. He never kissed an ugly girl.

Jonathan Grober
(dates unknown)

Jonathan Grober
Died dead sober.
Lord thy wonders never cease.

King Charles II
(1630–85)

God bless our good and gracious King,
Whose promise none relies on;
Who never said a foolish thing,
Nor ever did a wise one.

Thomas Fuller
(1608–61)
Church historian

~

Here lies Fuller's
Earth.

Charlotte Greer
(died 1900)

~

Here lies the body of Charlotte Greer,
Whose mouth would stretch from ear to ear.
Be careful as you tread this sod
For if she gapes, you're gone, by God!

Willie Michie
(18th century)

∼

Here lie Willie Michie's bones;
O Satan, when ye tak him,
Gie him the schoolin' of your weens,
For clever devils he'll mak them.

Colonel Francis Chartres
(died 1732)

∼

HERE continueth to rot
The body of Francis Chartres;
Who, with an INFLEXIBLE CONSTANCY
and INIMITABLE UNIFORMITY of life,
PERSISTED
In spite of AGE and INFIRMITIES,
In the practice of EVERY HUMAN VICE,
Excepting, PRODIGALITY and HYPOCRISY:
His insatiable AVARICE exempted him from the first,
His matchless IMPUDENCE from the second.

Nor was he more singular in the undeviating pravity
of his manners, than successful in accumulating
WEALTH:

For, without TRADE or PROFESSION,
Without TRUST of PUBLIC MONEY,
And without BRIBE-WORTHY SERVICE,
He acquired, or more properly created,
A MINISTERIAL ESTATE.

He was the only person of his time
Who cou'd CHEAT without the mask of HONESTY,
Retain his primeval MEANNESS when Possess'd of
TEN THOUSAND a year;
And, having daily deserv'd the GIBBET for what he
    did,
Was at last condemn'd to it for what he could not do.

O indignant reader!
Think not his life useless to mankind!
PROVIDENCE conniv'd at his execrable designs,
To give to after-ages a conspicuous PROOF and
    EXAMPLE
Of how small estimation is EXHORBITANT WEALTH
in the sight of GOD, by his bestowing it on the
most UNWORTHY of ALL MORTALS.

Name unknown
(died 1577)

~

While as I lived no house I had,
Now dead I have a grave.
In life I lived in loathsome lack,
Now dead I nothing crave.
In life I lived an exile poor,
Now death brings rest to me.
In life poor naked soul unclad,
Now clad in clods ye be.

Martha Dias
(1730–1800)

~

Here lies the body of Martha Dias,
Who was always uneasy and not over pious.
She liv'd to the age of threescore and ten,
And gave that to the worms she refus'd to the men.

Thomas Hood
(1798–1845)

~

He sang the song of the shirt . . .

Mike O'Day
(dates unknown)

~

This is the grave of Mike O'Day
Who died maintaining his right of way.
His right was clear, his will was strong.
But he's just as dead as if he'd been wrong.

Delia
(16th century)
~

Here Delia's buried at fourscore;
When young, a lewd, rapacious Whore,
Vain and expensive; but when old,
A pious, sordid, drunken Scold.

Name unknown
(18th century)
~

Here lies my poor wife, much lamented,
She is happy and I am contented.

Lord Coningsby
(18th century)
~

Here lies Lord Coningsby – be civil,
The rest God knows – so does the Devil.

Sir John Strange
(1696–1754)

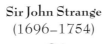

Here lies an honest lawyer, –
That is Strange.

Dorothy Parker
(1893–1967)

Excuse my Dust.

John Hewet and Sarah Drew
(died 1718)

~

Here lies John Hughes and Sarah Drew.
Perhaps you'll say, what's that to you?
Believe me, friend, much may be said
On this poor couple that are dead.
On Sunday next they should have married;
But see how oddly things are carry'd,
On Thursday last it rain'd and lighten'd,
These tender lovers sadly frighten'd
Shelter'd beneath the cocking hay
In hopes to pass the storm away.
But the bold thunder found them out
(Commission'd for that end no doubt)
And seizing on their trembling breath,
Consign'd them to the shades of death.
Who knows if 'twas not kindly done?
For had they seen the next year's sun,
A beaten wife and cuckold swain
had jointly curs'd the marriage chain.
Now they are happy in their doom,
For P. has wrote upon their tomb.

Wallace Ford
(1897–1966)
British actor

~

At last I get top billing.

Sir John Vanbrugh
(1664–1726)
St Stephen's Church, City of London

~

Under this stone, Reader, survey
Dead Sir John Vanbrugh's house of clay.
Lie heavy on him, Earth! for he
Laid many heavy loads on thee.

Tony Sympson
(1906–83)
Saucepan man in "Noddy in Toyland"

~

Inspired player of small parts

Dame Mary Page
(1672–1728)

~

Here lyes Dame Mary Page
Relict of Sir Gregory Page Bart
She departed this life March 4, 1728
In the 56th year of her age.

In 67 months she was tapped 66 times
Had taken away 240 gallons of water
without ever repining at her case
or ever fearing the operation.

Dr Keene
(18th century)

Here lies Dr Keene, the good Bishop of Chester,
Who eat up a fat goose, but could not digest her.

Viscount Castlereagh
(1769–1822)

Posterity will ne'er survey
A nobler grave than this:
Here lie the bones of Castlereagh:
Stop, traveller, and piss.

John Gay
(1685–1732)

~

Life is a jest and all things show it.
I thought so once; but now I know it.

Peg Rathly
(17th century)

~

Here lies Peg, that drunken sot,
Who dearly loved her jug and pot;
There she lies as sure can be,
She killed herself by drinking brandy.

Daniel Lambert
(1770–1809)

~

In memory of that prodigy in nature
Daniel Lambert
a native of Leicester,
who was possessed of an excellent and convivial mind
and in personal greatness
had no competitor.
He measured three feet one inch round the leg,
nine feet four inches round the body
and weighed 52 stones 11 lbs.
(14 lb to the stone).
As a testimony of respect,
this stone was erected by his
friends in Leicester.

Alexis Piron
(1689–1773)

~

Here lies Piron, a complete nullibiety,
Not even a fellow of a Learned Society.

Robert Dudley, Earl of Leicester
(16th century)

~

Here lieth the worthy warrior
Who never bloodied sword;
Here lieth the noble counsellor,
Who never held his word.

Here lieth his Excellency,
Who ruled all the state;
Here lieth the Earl of Leicester,
Whom all the world did hate.

Henry Hughes Cooper
(1759)

~

The left leg & part of the thigh
of Henry Hughes Cooper was
cut off & interr'd here
June 18th 1759

Martin Elphinstone
(18th century)

~

Here lieth Martin Elphinstone
Who with his sword did cut in sunder
The daughter of Sir Harry Crispe
who did his daughter marry.

She was fat and fulsome,
But men will sometimes
Eat bacon with their beans
And love the fat as well as lean.

Captain Underwood
(18th century)

~

Here lies free from blood and slaughter
Once Underwood — now under water.

Judge Ryneveld
(19th century)

~

Here lies in death, who living always lied,
A base amalgam of deceit and pride;
A wily African of monstrous shape,
The mighty Quinbus Flestrin of the Cape.
Rogue paramount, then thousand rogues among,
He rose and shone like phosphorus from dung;
The wolf and fox their attributes combined,
To form the odious features of his mind:
Where kennelled deep, by shame, by fear, unawed,
Lurk'd rapin, villainy, deceit, and fraud,
Hypocrisy, servility and lust;
A petty tyrant, and a Judge unjust,
Partial and stern, in every cause he tried,
He judged like Pilate, and like Pilate died.
Urged to despair, by crimes precluding hope,
He chose a bullet, to avoid a rope.
Consistent knave! his life in cheating passed,
He shot himself, to cheat the law at last.
Acme of crimes, self-murder crowned the whole,
And gave to worms his corpse – to fiends his soul.

Frederick Louis, Prince of Wales
(1707–51)
Eldest son of George II

~

Here lies Fred
Who was alive and is dead:
Had it been his father,
I had much rather;
Had it been his brother,
Still better than another;
Had it been his sister,
No one would have missed her;
Had it been the whole generation,
So much the better for the nation.
But since 'tis only Fred,
Who was alive and is dead,
There's no more to be said.

Peter Robinson
(19th century)

~

Here lies the preacher, judge and poet, Peter
Who broke the laws of God, and man, and metre.

Richard Hind
(18th century)

~

Here lies the body of Richard Hind,
Who was neither ingenious, sober, nor kind

Robert Southy
(19th century)

~

Beneath these poppies buried deep,
The bones of Bob the bard lie hid;
Peace to his manes; and may he sleep
As soundly as his readers did!

Through every sort of verse meandering,
Bob went without a hitch or fall,
Through epic, Sapphic, Alexandrine,
To verse that was no verse at all;

Till fiction having done enough,
To make a bard at least absurd,
And give his readers quantum suff,
He took to praising George the Third,

And now in virtue of his crown,
Dooms us, poor whigs, at once to slaughter;
Like donellan of bad renown,
Poisoning us all with laurel water.

And yet at times some awful qualms he
Felt about leaving honour's track;
And though he's got a butt of Malmsey,
It may not save him from a sack.

Death weary of so dull a writer,
Put to his books a finis thus.
Oh! may the earth on him lie lighter
Than did his quartos upon us!

Dr Chard
(19th century)

~

Here lies the corpse of Doctor Chard,
Who fill'd half of this churchyard.

Richard Burbage
(1567–1619)

~

Exit Burbage.

Hallenbeck family
(1950s)

~

The Family of Robert T. Hallenbeck.
None of us ever voted for
Roosevelt or Truman.

Martin Elginbrodde
(died 1862)

~

Here lie I, Martin Elginbrodde:
Have mercy o' my soul, Lord God,
As I wad do, were I Lord God
And ye were Martin Elginbrodde.

H.J. Daniel
(1818–89)

~

Here lies a bard, let epitaphs be true,
His vices many, and his virtues few;
Who always left religion in the lurch
But never left a tavern for a church,
Drank more from pewter than Pierian spring
And only in his cups was known to sing;
Laugh'd at the world, however it may blame,
And died regardless of his fate or fame.

John Edwards
(died 1904)

~

John Edwards who perished in a fire
None could hold a candle to him.

Anne Harrison
(1665–1745)

~

S. M. Anne Harrison,
well known by the name of NANNA RAN DAN,
who was chaste, but no prude;
& tho' free yet no harlot.
By principle virtuous,
by Education a Protestant;
her freedom made her liable to censure,
while her extensive charities made her esteemed.
Her tongue she was unable to control
but the rest of her members she kept in subjection.

Ann Jennings
(19th century)

Some have children, some have none:
Here lies the mother of twenty-one.

Unknown vicar
(18th century)

He was literally a father to all the children of
the parish.

Rosamond Clifford
(died 1177)
Mistress of King Henry II

In this tomb lies Rosamond,
the Rose of the world,
the fair, but not the pure.

Name unknown
(died 1701)
Droitwich

~

Here lie I and my three daughters,
All from drinking the Cheltenham waters.
While if we had kept to the Epsom salts,
We should not now be in these here vaults.

Margaret Ratcliffe
(17th century)

~

M arble weepe, for thou dost cover
A dead Beautie underneath thee,
R ich as Nature could bequeath thee;
G rant that no rude Hand remove her:
A ll the gazers on the skies
R ead not in fair heav'ns Storie,
E xpresser Truth, or truer Glorie
T han thy might in her bright Eyes.

R are as Wonder was her Wit,
A nd like Nectar, ever flowing;
T ill Time, strong by her bestowing,
C onquered hath both life and it:
L ife whose griefe was out of Fashion,
I n these Times. Few so have rued
F ate in a Brother. To conclude,
F or Wit, Feature and true Passion
E arth, thou hast not such another.

Sir Cowasji Jehangir Kt, C.S.I.
(19th century)
Old College, Edinburgh University

∿

The Peabody of the East.

John Green
(1604–32)

~

Stay reader drop upon this stone
One pitying tear and then be gone.
A handsome pile of flesh and blood
Is here sunk down to its first mud,
Which thus in Western rubbish lies
until the Eastern Star shall rise.

Thomas and Mary Bond
(died 1768)

~

Here lie the bodies
Of Thomas Bond and Mary his wife.
She was temperate, chaste and charitable;
BUT
She was proud, peevish, and passionate.
She was an affectionate wife, and a tender mother:
BUT
Her husband and child, whom she loved

Seldom saw her countenance without a disgusting
    frown,
Whilst she received visitors, whom she despised, with
    an endearing smile.
Her behaviour was discreet towards strangers;
BUT
Independent in her family.
Abroad her conduct was influenced by good breeding;
BUT
At home, by ill temper.
She was a professed enemy to flattery,
And was seldom known to praise or commend;
BUT
The talents in which she principally excelled,
Were differences of opinion and discovering flaws
    and imperfections.
She was an admirable economist,
And, without prodigality,
Dispensed plenty to every person in her family;
BUT
Would sacrifice their eyes to a farthing candle.
She sometimes made her husband happy with her
    good qualities;
BUT

Much more frequently miserable – with her many
    failings

Insomuch that in thirty years cohabitation he often
    lamented

That maugre of all her virtues,

He had not in the whole enjoyed two years of
    matrimonial comfort.

AT LENGTH

Finding that she had lost the affections of her
    husband,

As well as the regard of her neighbours,

Family disputes having been divulged by servants,

She died of vexation, July 20th 1768,

Aged 48 years.

Her worn out husband survived her four months and
    two days,

And departed this life, Nov. 28 1768.

Name unknown
(19th century)

~

Here lies my dear wife, a sad slattern and a shrew.
If I said I regretted her, I should lie too.

Dorothy Cecil
(died 1900s)

~

Dorothy Cecil unmarried
As yet.

John Bunn
(19th century)

~

Here lies John Bunn
Who was killed by a gun.
His name wasn't Bunn, but his real name was Wood,
But Wood wouldn't rhyme with gun,
So I thought Bunn should.

Name unknown
(19th century)

~

Here X lies dead, but God's forgiving,
And shows compassion to the livng.

Elizabeth Charlotte
(dates unknown)

~

Here lie the bones of Elizabeth Charlotte
Born a virgin, died a harlot.
She was aye a virgin at seventeen
A remarkable thing in Aberdeen.

John Randall
(1629–99)
Great Wolford, Warwickshire

∽

Here Old John Randall lies,
Who counting from his tale,
Lived three score years and ten,
Such virtue was in Ale.
Ale was his meat,
Ale was his drink,
Ale did his heart revive;
And if he could have drunk his Ale,
He still had been alive;
But he died January five.

John Macfarlane
(dates unknown)

∽

Erected to the memory of
John Macfarlane
Drowned in the Waters of Leith
By a few affectionate friends.

John Brown
(18th century)
Dentist

~

Stranger! Approach this spot with gravity!
John Brown is filling his last cavity.

Jemima Jones
(died 1803)

~

This is the last long resting place
Of Aunt Jemima Jones
Her soul ascended into space
Amidst our tears and groans
She was not pleasing to the eye
Nor had she any brain
And when she talked twas through her nose
Which gave her friends much pain
But still we feel that she was worth
The money that was spent
Upon the coffin, hearse and stone
(The funeral plumes were lent).

Thomas Vernon
(dates unknown)

~

Here lies the body of Thomas Vernon,
The only surviving son of Admiral Vernon.

James Andrewe
(died 1638)

~

JAMES ANDREWE
Anagram
Reede I was man

The Unknown Citizen
(To JS 07/M378)
This Marble Monument
Is Erected by the State

~

He was found by the Bureau of Statistics to be
One against whom there was no official complaint,
And all the reports on his conduct agree
That, in every modern sense of an old-fashioned
    word, he was a saint,
For in everything he did he served the Greater
    community.
Except for the War till the day he retired
He worked in a factory and never got fired,
But satisfied his employers, Fudge Motors Inc.
Yet he wasn't a scab or odd in his views,
For his Union reports that he paid his dues,
(Our report on his Union shows it was sound)
And our Social Psychology workers found
That he was popular in his work and liked a drink.
The Press are convinced that he bought a paper every
    day
And that his reactions to advertisements were
    normal in every way.

Policies taken out in his name prove that he was
    insured,
And his Health-card shows that he was once in
    hospital but left it cured.
Both Producers Research and High Grade Living
    declare
He was fully sensible to the advantages of the
    Instalment Plan
And had everything necessary to the Modern Man,
A phonograph, a radio, a car and a frigidaire.
Our researchers into Public Opinion are content
That he held the proper opinions for the time of year;
When there was peace, he was for peace; when there
    was a war, he went.
He was married, and added five children to the
    population,
Which our Eugenist says was the right number for a
    parent of his generation,
And our teachers report that he never interfered with
    their education.
Was he free? Was he happy? The question is absurd:
Had anything been wrong, we should certainly have
    heard.

Mary Broomfield
(1675–1755)

~

The chief concern of her life for the last
twenty-five years was to order and provide
for her funeral. Her greatest pleasure
was to think and talk about it. She lived
many years on a pension of 9d per week
and yet she saved £5, which at her own
request was laid out on her funeral.

Mr Jones
(19th century)

~

Here lies old Jones,
Who all his life collected bones,
Till Death, that grim and sorry spectre,
That all inspecting bone collector,
Boned poor Jones, so neat and tidy
Here he lies, all bona fide.

Martha Blewit
(died 1681)

~

Martha Blewit,
of the Swan Inn at Bathorn-End
in this Parish,
buried May 7th 1681:
was the wife of nine husbands successively,
but the ninth outlived her.
The Text to her Funeral Sermon was
"Last of all the Woman died also."